Just the Two of Us
Teens Write About Building Good Relationships

By Youth Communication

Edited by Al Desetta
with Nora McCarthy

Just the Two of Us

EXECUTIVE EDITORS
Keith Hefner and Laura Longhine

CONTRIBUTING EDITORS
Rachel Blustain, Kendra Hurley, Al Desetta,
Sheila Feeney, Laura Longhine, and Autumn Spanne

LAYOUT & DESIGN
Efrain Reyes, Jr. and Jeff Faerber

COVER ART
Shaun Shishido

Copyright © 2009 by Youth Communication ®

All rights reserved under International and Pan-American Copyright Conventions. Unless otherwise noted, no part of this book may be reproduced, stored in a retrieval system, or transmitted in any form or by any means, electronic, mechanical, photocopying, recording, or otherwise, without express written permission of the publisher, except for brief quotations or critical reviews.

For reprint information, please contact Youth Communication.

ISBN 978-1-933939-91-9

Second, Expanded Edition

Printed in the United States of America

Youth Communication ®
New York, New York
www.youthcomm.org

Table of Contents

Am I Ready For Love? *Hattie Rice* 11
    Hattie wants a romantic relationship but fears
    getting hurt.

Just the Two of Us, *Oumar Bowman* 16
    Oumar and Nina become as close as family.

Making a Fairy Tale Out of a Man, *Anonymous* 21
    When her boyfriend becomes aggressive, the writer
    starts to reevaluate their relationship.

When the Past Pops Up, Pay Attention, *Natasha Santos* 29
    A therapist discusses how emotional baggage from the
    past can affect relationships.

Opening Up to My Shorty, *Antwaun Garcia* 34
    A former player, Antwaun discovers it feels good to get
    close to one person.

Reaching Out to My Enemy, *Chantel Clark* 39
    Once archenemies, Chantel and Kim realize they have
    more in common than they ever imagined.

Want a Friend? Be a Friend! *Antwaun Garcia* 44
    Antwaun looks at ways to make and keep good friends.

Contents

My Sister and Me, *Cynthia Orbes* 48
    Cynthia and her sister Natalie have different strategies for protecting themselves in relationships.

Loving and Losing, *Anonymous* 53
    The writer bonds with a girl named Katy, who helps him get his life under control.

Black and Blue, *Zoraida Medina* 60
    Tony hits Zoraida so severely she has to seek an order of protection.

How to Know if a Relationship Is Good for You 65

For Love or Money, *Erica Harrigan* 68
    Erica feels used by her boyfriend, and decides she deserves something better.

Player No More, *Rosheed Wellington* 73
    Rosheed is cynical and cautious about relationships— until he meets someone special.

In Search of Myself, *Seandrea Evans* 79
    Because of her past, Seandrea is out of touch with her feelings and doesn't feel comfortable in relationships.

My First Friend, *Hattie Rice* 86
    Hattie suffers from "social phobia," but her friend Amanda is able to break through the walls.

Playing to Win, *Fred Wagenhauser* 91
Fred is afraid to commit to one girl, but decides on a
new path after a girl he's dating cheats on him.

Learning To Love Again, *Shaniqua Sockwell* 98
Shaniqua develops a more realistic view of love.

FICTION SPECIAL: Lost and Found, *Anne Schraff* 103

Teens: How to Get More Out of This Book 112

How to Use This Book in Staff Training 113

Teachers and Staff: How to Use This Book In Groups 114

Credits 116

About Youth Communication 117

About the Editors 120

More Helpful Books from Youth Communication 122

Introduction

Oumar Bowman meets Nina at a job-training program at his foster care agency. They flirt, start dating, and eventually grow very close.

"Maybe one of the reasons we're so tight is that we don't have too many others to rely on," Oumar writes. "Nina and I try to fill in what's missing in each other's lives, and we've become each other's family."

They grow so close that they even seem to know what the other is thinking. "It feels good when you have someone to lean on, especially if you've spent most of your life relying on yourself," Oumar says, but then adds, almost as a warning to himself: "If your relationship doesn't make it, you still always have you."

Omar touches on two themes that surface throughout the 17 true stories in *Just the Two of Us*—young people's desire to connect emotionally with others through friendship or romance, and their simultaneous need to forge an identity outside a relationship. That boundary can be difficult to maintain.

Oumar and Nina are lucky to have found each other, but knowing how to create and maintain healthy relationships—and avoid bad ones—isn't easy for anyone. It can be especially difficult for teens in foster care. Abondonment, or being let down by people you love, can leave you emotionally vulnerable or unwilling to trust others.

For example, in "My Sister and Me," Cynthia Orbes writes that she and her sister Natalie have suffered multiple losses. As a result, Natalie keeps people at a distance in relationships to avoid getting hurt, while Cynthia is afraid to be alone and gets close too fast.

"Natalie and I would probably both be better off if we could be more like each other," Cynthia writes. "I think she'd be happy if she really trusted someone enough to fall in love. And I'm trying her method of not falling in love that easily."

For Seandrea Evans, growing up with an unpredictable mother, and then in numerous foster homes, meant she constantly had to adjust to new personalities. That's made it hard for her to know herself, especially in new relationships:

"I act so many different ways that it's hard to know how I want to respond in certain situations, especially with my boyfriend. When he tells me, 'Be yourself,' I don't know what that really means."

What makes *Just the Two of Us* so helpful for teens and staff is that the writers begin to find some answers. Rosheed Wellington and Antwaun Garcia both tire of using girls for sex and begin to look for mature and serious relationships in which they can express their feelings. Other writers give up the fantasy that a relationship will make them happy and instead look inside themselves to build their self-esteem.

"Now I know what I want in a relationship and I'm not in as much of a rush to wrap my life around my boyfriend," says one writer. "I'm trying not to depend on Prince Charming for my happiness."

The writers also interview therapists and counselors to gain insight into how to build strong relationships, and recognize harmful ones. We hope these stories will help you reflect on the relationships in your own life, and think about the kinds of relationships you'd like to have in the future.

In the following stories, names have been changed: *Just the Two of Us*, *Black and Blue*, *Loving and Losing*, and *Making a Fairy Tale Out of a Man*.

Dante Gutierrez

Am I Ready For Love?

By Hattie Rice

Here's the problem: I've never had a man, never had a kiss. I've never gotten TLC (tender loving care) on TLC (tables, ladders, and chairs).

When my girls ask why, I kick it corny and old school: "Books before boys because boys bring babies." But the real reason is more complicated.

For one thing, the girls I know let their boys come first and seem to find nothing but trouble. Their boyfriends hit them and leave them on the brink of tears. They cheat. The boys do not appreciate the sacrifices my friends make.

Then I'm left putting my friends back together like a jigsaw puzzle. I see their hurt and it scares me. They become so emotionally attached that they allow their men to make them weak while depending on them for strength.

Just the Two of Us

The way I see it, love is a risk that my girlfriends have not benefited from taking. I don't want to make the same mistakes, end up disrespected, have someone violate my trust, and find myself so lost in the idea of love that I accept them back and forget myself.

Seems like love is overrated, a promise rarely kept.

But as Shakespeare said, "Tis better to have loved and lost than to never have loved at all." I sincerely believe that. Love may bring the greatest pains but it can also give us our greatest joys. I want to experience it for myself. But I have to wonder: am I ready to love?

I feel that I have a lot to offer in a relationship. I'm a good listener. I'm also strong and sensitive. I usually can sense what people need. I don't believe I'll become emotional baggage for my partner because I try to be as independent as possible.

So I have a lot to give. What scares me is what I'll receive. I fear I'll love too deeply, and then how will I let go if all I had to give is disrespected? How will I go on? Plus, I have such high expectations that one thing is certain: I'm going to be let down and it's going to be hard. I can seriously see myself having a nervous breakdown.

My fear that love could destroy me comes from my relationship with my family, especially my mom. Since I was 12, I've felt my mom's schizophrenia as a weight on me. I still feel responsible for her, even though my helpless attempts to take care of her couldn't make her recover.

I loved my mom so much I gave up on myself. I dropped out of school, fell into a deep depression, and thought my life had no value apart from my ability to care for my mother.

I also loved my dad and trusted him to look out for my best interests. Let's just say my best interests were not served by my father dropping jokes on my "linebacker" shoulders or allowing my mom to spend our food money on crack.

Since coming into foster care at age 14, I've shielded myself from love because I know that those you love the most are also the people who can hurt you the most. My power and control to protect myself from love protects me from being vulnerable and susceptible to pain. I tell myself, "I can't go through loving and losing again." I barely got through it with my family.

When I think of dating, I find myself intertwining my experiences with my parents with my fears (and hopes) for falling in love with a boy. I'm scared to love, scared of my love being misused, scared of the effect a person I care about could have on me.

My experiences in foster care haven't exactly improved my ability to trust, either. Turns out it's hard to find trustworthiness in others.

One time I met a psychiatrist I felt comfortable with and we talked about my family history. I told him my mom hears voices and is so paranoid she pulls down the shades (like people really want to spy on her life). It was hard for me to tell that to him—and then he accused me of lying! I'm sure I need therapy to get over what I've been through, but my experience with that psychiatrist sure didn't help me reach out.

With all the untrustworthy people I've known, I feel uncomfortable opening up. I'm

Seems like love is overrated, a promise rarely kept.

scared that if I meet a guy I like, his first reaction will be to judge, and my chain reaction will be to swing (just kidding). It doesn't help to be in foster care. People ask me basic get-to-know-you questions about family and I feel like I'm being meticulously ice grilled.

Scary as love is, though, I don't want to be lonely. Loneliness is something I'm all too familiar with. Loneliness shortly leads to despair, turmoil, sinking into oblivion. . . (maybe not all that, but I am a drama queen, so too much alone time just isn't healthy).

When I think of spending my days without love, I remember when I was younger. I was an outcast. I had no friends. I was left to deal with my loneliness and social problems alone. When you're a kid you're supposed to cry on your mom's shoulder, but instead she was crying on mine.

I had the happiest moment of my life not too long ago. It was 9 a.m. and we were slowly creeping up 2nd Avenue with the rain beating at the window of the car. We were conversing loudly—shouting. Then my mom tells us to shush. My dad wants to know what's good, and I'm with him, and then we see a tear stream down my mom's face. It was the first time I'd seen her cry.

She managed to utter, "I don't hear anything," and immediately I started to tear up. Nobody said anything. There was a deadly silence as my mom felt a sensation—quiet—she hadn't felt since about age 12. I wished in that instant that my mom could get well and provide me the love and nurturing that I desire. It felt like my wish was getting closer, but the moment was gone in 60 seconds.

My fear that love could destroy me comes from my relationship with my family.

So you can see how I'm thirsty for love. If some man tried to love me, I'm afraid my thirst would come out so strong that either nothing could quench it, or I could never give up the little sip I had no matter what happened. I want to find someone who listens, understands, and respects my opinions. And I want to provide the same support for somebody, but how?

My social skills are not the best. I have a hard time making friends. So how am I going to draw boys in and get one to love me?

My best friend has been trying to hook me up with different guys for the longest. I'm fine with my male friends, but when a guy wants more I put out less. It's almost as if I make them not like me. My uneasiness comes off as rudeness.

Also, for a while, I had crushes on boys that just weren't realistic. You know, thugs. But recently I started thinking I might actually want to get close to someone who is a good person—

someone competent, someone who can read and write.

I don't how it will happen or when, but maybe it's one step closer for me to simply admit that I want a man. I want to be loved, and I want to love someone. I long for a time when I feel comfortable around someone else, when I can be myself with a man and just chill. That's what love seems to promise to me—it could give me a place where I belong in this world, starting with the person I belong with.

Hattie was 18 when she wrote this story. She attended SUNY Binghamton.

Just the Two of Us

By Oumar Bowman

When I first met my girlfriend Nina, I thought that she was quite dimed out, with a right-side dimple that matched my left-side dimple. She had a nice shape, nice size, nice thighs, nice eyes. I was attracted but, I must admit, I was also distracted.

I was not involved with another, but I was also not in a rush to be loved. My past relationships had gotten me stressed. My past girlfriends had had so many problems—family problems, personal problems, just problems period—which kept our relationships from ascending.

I met Nina at a job-training program through my foster care agency. She almost always tried to let me know that she liked me. She would say hello every time she saw me, and she would sit next to me in the class and make jokes to impress me. Nina even threw water on me one time (she was trying to flirt), but I just walked away. I kept our relationship on a hi-and-bye status. She didn't appreciate that.

But as the weeks went by, I became crazily attracted to her. I liked and respected her because I could tell she was very smart and observant. Nina wouldn't speak if she wasn't involved in the conversation, but she'd watch what was going on. I liked that she seemed truthful and good at analyzing. What's more, I thought she was good looking enough to be my wife. Nina made me want to hold up a big torch in the night, proclaiming her loveliness.

Others were charmed and bewitched by her aura. But apparently she held the slot for yours truly. The fact that she rejected those cats made me like her even more.

That's when my feelings began to show. I wouldn't let others speak to her and I wouldn't join in their chauvinistic games, like when the guys in the program would attack girls' hair, sneakers, jewelry, and looks in general. I left that type of topic to the non-exclusive cats.

Nina and I try to fill in what's missing in each other's lives, and we've become each other's family.

Then one week when not too many people came to the program, Nina and I were sitting in the big blue agency van, waiting to go home after a meeting, and I asked her, "Are you going to the barbecue on Saturday?"

"No," she said.

Then I got to the topic. "Are you involved at the moment?"

"No," she said.

"Then what's up?" I said.

"Are you sure?" she said.

"Positive," I said.

Then Nina told me something that took my heart away. She said, "You know something? That's funny. I been feeling you, but now I know you're real about this."

On the way home we talked about almost everything that

would bring us closer, like what type of relationships we were in before. And we made sure that we were the only ones each of us was seeing. After we dropped her off I did some thinking, and the decision I made was official.

Nina and I have been dating each other for only five months, but in that short time we've gotten real tight. It's strange how sometimes we even seem to know what the other one is thinking. Like if we think about calling each other on the phone, or even something so simple as asking each other for a drink of water, we find it's already being done.

We depend on each other, and when we're together we're totally into one another. We can tell, just from looking into each other's eyes. It's a certain vibe I get from our relationship that makes me know I love her.

Sometimes we even seem to know what the other one is thinking.

Maybe one of the reasons we're so tight is that we don't have too many others to rely on. Both of our biological parents died when we were younger. Very few of her family members are still alive, and mine I'm not too close to. Nina and I try to fill in what's missing in each other's lives, and we've become each other's family.

You can see this in the way Nina and I tend to baby and take care of each other, kind of like a parent would for a child. For example, if my hair is nappy she'll comb it for me. If I'm cold, she'll go to her house to get me one of her sweaters. When I was weak and sick, she kissed me so gently that it made me reminisce about places I've never been.

She acts just like a mother when she helps me save money. I appreciate that because I'm not good at keeping money, just spending it. I usually spend my money on unnecessary items of unworthy preferences or on expensive gifts. But she tells me to save in order to have money for important things, like clothing or household items I might want when I've got my own place, or just saving for my future in general.

This type of managing makes me feel special. Besides, I can always rely on her if I need some money, because she keeps some of mine for me. So if I need a certain item, or if we have somewhere special to go, I don't have to worry about my financial status.

And sometimes she turns to me like family, too. There was a time when I was weak from a head injury, but I still took her all the way home to make sure she had a safe and comfortable journey. Or when I have a weekend pass, she comes over and I make breakfast for her, like a regular couple.

I act kind of like a father when it comes to studying. I think Nina needs to focus a little more on her education, so now I'm trying to get her into the habit of writing.

From what I can tell, she is good at depicting and she has a good imagination. I've encouraged her to put whatever is in her head on paper and bring it to life. Now she writes for me every night before she goes to bed.

I can't front, Nina and I have been in a few arguments. The fact that we rely on each other so strongly can sometimes be stressful, especially when we need something and we can't scope each other out. For instance, sometimes when we've negotiated a date and time to see each other, and she might be running a little late, I immediately begin to ponder and panic. And when finally I do see her…well, you know she has to hear it from me.

Or when she calls for me and I'm not at home, I'm going to hear it, too, when I do get in. It's like we're afraid of losing each other, so we act kind of possessive to keep each other in check.

Plus, sometimes the group home atmosphere gets the better of us. Like when we have to deal with jealous residents gossiping about our relationship, or saying stuff about the person we're dating, just to make things rocky and uneven. The gossip is one reason some residents don't want to date other kids in care. But I think it's worth it because every time Nina and I do fight, afterward we can barely let each other go.

Just the Two of Us

It feels good when you have someone to lean on, especially if you've spent most of your life relying on yourself. If your relationship doesn't make it, you still always have you. But it's nice to have someone there, that special person, who can hold you down when you need it, and even when you don't.

Life may have much more in store for me and Nina. But I hope that ours is a situation where love will outlast time. I truly believe that we just might stay together.

Oumar was 19 when he wrote this story.

Making a Fairy Tale Out of a Man

By Anonymous

We were both stressed out as we left the house. "Why did you speak to my mom about our problems?" James asked angrily.

"Who am I supposed to talk to if you don't ever listen to me?" I responded. He turned his back to me, clearly pissed.

Then he gripped my arms, shoved me against the door, and gave me a look that I'd never seen in the couple of years we'd been together. "Don't ever talk back again," he whispered.

My mind went dizzy. I fell into deep silence. He looked away. The night ended with him going to a party and me stuck on the subway, replaying the whole scene. A whole bunch of negative thoughts came into my mind. "Is this becoming an abusive relationship? Would I be better off alone?"

My family has a history of abusive relationships. My grandfather abused his wife and kids. My Aunt Jenny's husband abused her. (She divorced him.) My mother got into an abusive relationship with my father, who abused my sister and me, too. He clearly viewed women as trash, and we all carried the bruises and scars to prove it.

My grandmother stayed with her abusive husband because she believed her kids needed a father, but when her children were teens she left and took them with her. She's never taken another hit or insult from a man again.

She's now in a relationship with a wonderful man who does almost anything to make her happy. He cooks dinner for her and they go out to the senior center together all the time.

But my grandmother still looks back with regret on ever staying with her ex-husband, and she keeps her guard up when it comes to men. Not a day goes by without her "All Men Are Dogs" speech, because she wants to protect my sister and me.

Even so, I don't want to end up alone like most of the women in my family. Love and passion seem worth the risk. I don't want my life to be forever overshadowed by my rough childhood with my father. I want to learn to trust and depend on someone else. I want to know that I can be safe with a boyfriend, and that not all men are bad.

James was my first boyfriend. His laugh attracted me to him. I was about 13 years old and had joined a teen program with my cousins. At the time, I was adjusting to foster care and dealing with memories of my father's abuse, along with the usual teen concerns. At the program, I felt shy and self-conscious and sat in a corner worrying about what the rest of the world thought about me.

One day as I was fighting with my sorrows, I was disturbed by a group of kids laughing up a storm. I wondered, "What the hell is so funny?" I looked up to see James' mesmerizing smile. It made me happy, but jealous. Smiling was something I hadn't done in a long time.

I guess the saying "opposites attract" is true because he was everything I wasn't—funny, outspoken, and happy. As days went by I observed him. I wanted to be him. I wanted to share his happiness.

About a year later my sadness slowly drifted away. My cousin set up a date with James for me, and I got the courage to go. Right away, we clicked. I wasn't shy around him.

We slowly walked down the beautiful streets of Manhattan, holding hands and admiring the uniqueness of each building and the lights. Most of all, we were admiring each other. He said everything right, and I had a warm feeling around him.

His punches felt like an introduction, like there'd be more pain to come.

After that we began having four-hour phone conversations that ended with my grandma interrupting the call. Days when we hung out, I would rest my head on his shoulder, listening to him recount endless adventures in school or around his neighborhood. Sometimes he would go on and on, blabbering about God knows what. His hugs and kisses would put me in a deep spellbinding dream.

But one night I saw that he had darkness inside him, too. He received a phone call from his father, and as they talked his smile fell into a frown. He held my hands tightly and I looked deep into his eyes as tears fell slowly across his face. His father was explaining that he'd be away for a while, since his mom and dad were divorcing. His grip grew tighter as more tears poured down.

When he got off the phone I kissed him, knowing that James needed my comfort, my arms around him, and my shoulder to lean on. It was exhilarating to feel wanted and needed. I held him, not wanting to let go.

Our relationship bloomed like a rose. Sadly, as the months went by, the petals slowly began to fall.

*E*very relationship has its ups and downs, but in our second year together James began to change. Our relationship did, too.

For some reason, he wanted to be a gangster. James is an intelligent young man who can accomplish anything he puts his mind to, but he began to savor the negative vibes the streets throw out. James' new activities were drugs and getting into trouble with his friends.

When I asked him about college, he just shrugged his shoulders and looked away. I figured it was a phase and he'd get over it, but after a while I thought to myself, "How much can a girl take?"

A few times, James took his anger out on me. One time we were play fighting in the middle of the living room, pretending we were in a boxing ring. We did that a lot, but this time was different. James became more aggressive. He hit me rapidly on my leg. Each blow made me feel weak, but anger made me competitive enough to hit him back forcefully, too.

My hits seemed to have no effect on him, so I grew even madder. Then he hit me near my throat and I fell down, out of breath. This monster didn't even help me up. Flashbacks of my abusive father pounding his punches deep into my flesh, just waiting for me to fall, appeared before my eyes. Tears ran down my face.

His punches felt like an introduction, like there'd be more pain to come.

I went in the bathroom to see if I had any bruises and looked in the mirror. I forced a smile. I was tired of being depressed, angry, confused—everything but happy. But I didn't want to show my feelings to someone who'd hurt me.

Coming out of the bathroom with my fixed face, I decided that James and I should talk. I'd faced bigger monsters than this, and this wasn't James' usual behavior, anyway. It was obvious that he was upset and taking his anger out on me.

All I wanted was an apology. But when I reached the living

room, he was already reaching for the door. "Why are you leaving?" I asked. "You wanted me to," he said, leaving me dumbfounded. Actually, I wanted him to stay and explain himself, not leave me fighting with my thoughts. I ran to catch him, but he was gone.

Sitting in my living room, I replayed that "All Men Are Dogs" speech over and over. I thought, "My grandma is right," and wondered, "Will I ever trust a man?" I hated that he could do or say things that led me back to being that helpless little girl in the corner, fighting her thoughts.

I called him the next day and asked him, "Why did you hit me?"

"Because you hit me," he said. I fell silent and he began to hum a cheerful tune, as if he were carefree.

When I mentioned the subject again, he quickly said, "Can we talk about something else?" As with all our arguments, we settled it his way, which was, "Drop it!" I tried to.

I knew my relationship with James was positive in many ways. I felt happier and more confident, and I also began to be more independent and to make friends.

But I also knew that ignoring things instead of talking them out would eventually lead to our downfall. I blamed myself for some of our problems communicating. I have a hard time trusting people, especially men, and I didn't really open up to him or connect with him the way I wanted to.

As we neared the end of our second year together, I sometimes felt like I didn't even know James anymore. He got arrested a few times, and became more aggressive and moody with me. I kept our conversations simple to avoid arguments, but sometimes our conversations ended with him hanging up, or insulting me and cursing me out.

Once James even told me he was cheating on me, but I didn't want to believe it. I told myself, "He's just saying that because he's angry and wants to hurt me." We dropped the subject, but I never forgot what he said.

For a long time I didn't want to break up, because I had the feeling that all boys are the same and this might be as good as it gets. It didn't help that my aunt tortured me every time we went shopping. In the lingerie section, she'd buy a thong or a whole bunch of sexy underwear and then turn to me, sighing, "I don't know why I'm buying this. The only person going to see this is me."

On Valentine's Day she bought herself teddy bears with hearts and the words "I love you" on them. She'd say, "I bought this for myself since nobody loves me."

[DROP CAP] Thinking about my aunt and mother's bad experiences with men, I'd get sad. The women in my family are beautiful, sensitive, loving, and emotional. I worried that if I couldn't make a relationship work with James, I'd end up alone.

I knew that ignoring things instead of talking them out would eventually lead to our downfall.

I also didn't trust my reactions to James' mean behavior. I knew I viewed the majority of men as perverts and abusers, so how accurately could I judge how he treated me? It freaked me out when a daughter sat on her father's lap. If any guys approached me I got disgusted, assuming they just want the hit and run.

But every time my sweet James gently lay down next to me and held on to me, the feeling of comfort and safety felt irreplaceable. I never wanted to lose that feeling, even when everything else about the relationship felt wrong.

Finally, though, I began to think, "I don't know what I'm trying do, staying with this boy for so long. What keeps me holding on? I'm holding on to something that isn't even there anymore." I wanted us to help and support each other, but that didn't seem possible.

I was trying to make a fairy tale out of him instead of being realistic and putting my real feelings first. Looking back, I can't believe what I put up with.

Finally, we broke up when a new Prince Charming came along and swept me off my feet. We started off as friends, and once our friendship gave me a taste of what a good relationship could feel like, I got tired of how James treated me. He was in and out of jail and on house arrest. I could see he wasn't about to mature.

I didn't want to deal with his cranky ways anymore, so I told him, "Out with the old and in with the new."

I try not to look back on my experience with James with regret. I just try to retrace my actions and learn from them. I look back at our arguments and I see that I've grown up and changed. Now I know that if a relationship feels angry and hurtful, I'm wasting my time. Next time I'll leave.

I'm pretty sure his intention was never to hurt me, although he did hurt me, and the way he treated me left scars. I've noticed that with Prince Charming, I'm too aggressive sometimes. I fear letting myself get hurt again, and want Prince Charming to know that I won't take any abuse.

I try to view my relationship now as just practice for the future. At 17, I'm still too young to really get caught up in a serious relationship. Besides, the biggest mistake the women in my family made was trying to find their happiness in the hands of someone else. James couldn't give me his happiness. My happiness needs to come from inside.

Now I know what I want in a relationship and I'm not in as much of a rush to wrap my life around my boyfriend. I'm trying not to depend on Prince Charming for my happiness. Writing stories, reading, and hanging out with friends and family all make me happy. So does spending time by myself and doing well in school. My new boyfriend doesn't confuse and distract me from my goals in life, but supports me.

Like my grandma, I've found out that there are good men out there. The women in my family didn't carry a curse or just have

Just the Two of Us

bad luck with men. They just made bad choices. They got caught up instead of putting their own priorities first. Just because my mom and my aunts chose men who hurt them doesn't mean I will end up following in their footsteps, as long as I learn from what they—and what I—did wrong.

The writer was 17 when she wrote this story.
She graduated from high school and went to Lehman College.

Michael Aurello

When the Past Pops Up, Pay Attention

By Natasha Santos

We enter relationships—any relationship—with baggage from our past. Whether we'd like to admit it or not, our pasts can often come up in our day-to-day dealings with loved ones. Certain touches or tones make us unreasonably defensive or angry because we're reminded of times when similar gestures were meant to harm us. For instance, one time when someone told me I was lying, I completely flipped because it reminded me of my foster mother, who would often accuse me of lying.

To find out how we can break the patterns we've grown up with, I talked with therapist Rebecca Weston, clinical director of the Brooklyn Children's Psychotherapy Project.

Q: How can past experiences affect teens' romantic relationships?

A: We learn how we deserve to be treated through seeing our parents' relationships. We also learn how to be intimate with other people through family, for better or for worse. If we're very close to a parent that has difficulty parenting, is gone a lot, or is abusive, we learn that love might involve violence, pain, or rejection.

Q: How do you know when a relationship is positive or unhealthy?

A: Good relationships make you feel confident to pursue goals important to you. Does the relationship empower you? Does it make you feel healthy and happy in school, work, job, home? If yes, it's a good, healthy relationship, and you should hang on to it.

Unhealthy relationship are almost the opposite. The most obvious unhealthy relationships involve physical violence or forced sexual or physical intimacy. Violence can be physical (you get hurt), emotional (you begin to feel you don't deserve respect), or threats to your safety (you're afraid that the person may hurt you or a loved one).

If the relationship corrodes or undermines the way you feel in other parts of your life—if you begin to feel isolated, afraid to talk about the relationship, disconnected from friends, or pressured to be a certain way that just doesn't feel right—then you don't want to continue it.

Q: Is it a given that our relationships will turn out like the relationships we had growing up? How can we change them?

A: No, I don't think it's inevitable. Unfortunately, we are told, "If you were abused as a kid, you'll be abusive." That can set you up to feel that there's nothing you can do to help yourself. You can make changes in the relationships you choose. But it's not easy. We have models in our heads from early childhood, but we can make decisions and we can consciously decide to change.

The best way to change your pattern is to look back and face your past. There's no way to avoid a painful reckoning with your past. Don't shove it aside and say, "It's not going to affect me." It affects you whether or not you want it to.

Take a look at what happened in your past. Be thoughtful: how does that make me feel about myself? How am I reacting to those things now? Look at it, with a friend, counselor, or mentor in a safe environment.

Q: Are there signs that you shouldn't date someone?

A: There are certainly red flags. If you've just met them and they're asking for your address and contact information, or they're not giving you very much room, or if they want to rush into sex, something is wrong. If they're not interested in you as a person, that's not good.

If you know them mostly through partying or drinking, or know they have a history of being with a lot of different people very quickly, that can be a sign that they're not safe to be with.

There's no way to avoid a painful reckoning with your past. It affects you whether or not you want it to.

Be mindful of what you feel inside. If you feel a little bit uncomfortable, feel pressure to behave a certain way, or feel pushed, pay attention to that feeling, regardless of what other people say or how it might feel to reject that person.

You have a well-tuned internal radar. If someone does not feel safe for whatever reason, you're usually right about that. If something inside is telling you that something is not right, you should listen to that caution.

Q: Sometimes I notice that people blow things out of proportion. Like, say you grew up being accused of being a thief and your boyfriend says he's missing a CD. That can turn into a huge fight. Why?

A: If in the past you were frequently being accused of something, or told that the abuse was your fault, like, "It's your fault that I hit you," or were automatically blamed for things that went wrong, you might end up adopting a view of the world like, "I can't trust anyone because they'll think I'm bad."

You're primed to be blamed or hurt, so when someone does make a casual statement, the whole history comes back. You think, "I can't handle it anymore, people always blame me." And you blow up. It can be hard to sort out the present moment from the whole history of your feelings, because your emotions are all confused.

Q: If you notice past issues coming up, how can you deal with them?

A: Noticing that your past is still with you is a great first step. The most common thing we do is tell ourselves the past doesn't matter. But it does.

Once you notice a pattern, the next step is talking to the person who it's coming up with and saying things like, "I think I overreacted because of these reasons, and I'm sorry about that, I'm going to try to deal with that past situation."

Then you can speak to a close friend, therapist, or counselor about what happened in the past and how you think it's connected to troubles you're having in the present. You can also help yourself by keeping a writing journal. Keep track of when and why the past comes back up. Like, "Whenever someone is late to meet me, what comes into my head is my dad never showing up. When it happens, I need to remember it doesn't mean I'm rejected and abandoned, they're just late." You can get to know your own pattern.

Q: Should you try to deal with your past in a relationship or should you deal with yourself and then get in a relationship?

A: Both can work. I don't think people should ever be afraid to get into a relationship. A healthy relationship can make you feel like, "I've got someone in my corner." That can help you deal with the past.

Sometimes, though, our pasts become so present in our heads that we only pursue abusive relationships or we screw up the good ones. In that case, it might be good to avoid relationships. You avoid messing up your life further while you try to deal with yourself.

Q: How do you know when you're ready for a relationship, and when you are not?

A: You don't always know. The most important thing is whether you feel that the person is someone you can be honest with. Like, if you've never had sex, are you comfortable admitting that to the person? If you are going to have sex, do you feel comfortable talking about the need to use protection? If the answers are no, I think you're not ready for a sexual relationship. Safe exploration of sexuality is not a bad thing, but you have to be ready to say, "I don't want to go further than this," or, "I'm scared about this."

Q: How can you deal with an abusive relationship?

A: Girls and young women tend to feel they don't deserve any better, so they either ignore abuse and hope it goes away, or feel isolated and keep it a secret. Sometimes people don't even know the relationship is abusive. Many times people don't seek help because they feel ashamed or feel like they're bad.

If you're in an abusive relationship, that doesn't mean something is wrong with you. It's not something to be ashamed of. It's common. Seek out help from a friend, a counselor, a social worker or therapist. People are there to help you out, to give you support and confidence. You do deserve better. Even if you've done things wrong, you don't deserve to be treated in an abusive way.

Natasha was 17 when she wrote this story. She later attended the University of New Orleans.

Opening Up to My Shorty

By Antwaun Garcia

Once in a while someone finally grows up and realizes what he wants. In my case, I went from being what you would call a pimp, a playa, someone who doesn't care about other people's feelings, to someone who is trying hard to settle down and be caring.

In all of my previous relationships I have cheated on a female with one or numerous other females. I didn't care too much about their feelings. I used females like a boy uses a toy.

Back in those days I used to have what I called "a phase" with a female. I would gas her head up like I needed her, like she was everything to me. (It was easy for me to tell girls nice things when I didn't mean them.) Then, poof, out of nowhere I'd let her know it was over. I could never face rejection, so I would hand it out before it came to me.

I would toss her number away, toss her letters, toss any pics of us, too. Kind of cold-hearted, I know, but it's the truth.

I would have females depressed thinking about me, wondering what I might be doing. My way of getting over a female was to just bag another one. Then, once again, after about a month, it was "bye-bye-bye."

I knew I didn't want to be like two of my boys, who were almost devastated because their girls left them. I'd hear cats in the streets complaining, "My girl left me." But that wasn't my way.

But after a while, I started getting annoyed at females who only cared how thick my pockets were. I wanted to settle down, to have a wifey to go places with and to miss when she's not with me.

Now, believe it or not, I think I have found that one. At the time we started talking, I was talking to five other girls, and she was talking to some cornball around her way. We were both tired of these corny people and wanted something serious. I will admit, I wasn't planning to be faithful to her at first. But she opened my eyes to the fact that she wasn't a dummy I would talk to and get my way with.

Now I have been dating her for the past 10 months, and to be honest they have been the best 10 months I have ever spent with any girl. She is mad

I could never face rejection, so I would hand it out before it came to me.

cool and mad funny. She has a great personality and is a very good listener. One thing about being a foster care kid is that you have a lot of drama going on, and you always need someone to listen to you and to talk with. Normally I don't talk to anyone, but my shorty has always opened her ear to me.

One week, we were talking on the phone from 10 at night to 4 in the morning when we both had to be at school early the next day. It wasn't those boring convos like, "The sky is blue, and the grass is green." We were really talking, really getting to know one another, really laughing the whole six or seven hours on the phone. I had never done that with any female before.

I couldn't get enough of this girl. When we had class together we would sit next to one another and talk through the whole class, or write notes and crack jokes. Afterwards we would get something to eat up the block at the bagel shop, and then I would walk her to the bus. We did that from February to the end of the school year.

What's real interesting is we have nothing in common, yet we are so compatible. She loves bacon. I hate pork. She loves horror films. I think they are corny and prefer a comedy or action film. She listens to rock and roll, and I listen to r&b and rap. Yet we still find similarities within one another.

And over the last 10 months she has always been there for me, no matter what. I have been through some tough times, and she stood by me through it all. She listened about my life and past. She couldn't believe how I survived what I've been through. It kind of left her speechless. But telling her about my past helped her understand why I am the person I am. She loves me for who I am.

The main problem I have with her and most females I've liked is letting my feelings show. Don't get me wrong, I've told females what they want to hear, but usually when I don't mean it. It's hard for me to tell my feelings when they're real. After all, I have kept my feelings bottled up since I was 10, the year two of my best friends died. They were the only two people I confided my feelings in. When I lost them, I felt like I couldn't talk to anyone else, and not talking about my feelings became a habit.

But with my shorty, I wanted to tell her my feelings. It just seemed like a big risk. What if I told her how I felt and we soon deaded things? Then I might feel mad and stupid for showing her my vulnerable side. I might be heartbroken, or feel pitiful and depressed.

But I knew I'd feel just as bad if the relationship ended and I never told her how I felt, or, worse, if it ended because I never told her how I felt. I decided that growing in relationships is all about showing people how you feel, and taking a chance by trusting them with your soft side.

Even if there are grimy people in the world, that didn't mean my shorty was one of them, and that I couldn't work at letting my feelings show, at my own pace, to make our relationship even better. And I wanted to get better at showing my feelings not just for my shorty, but because I wanted to be able to show my feelings to my family, too, especially my sister. For most of my life, my pride and stubbornness and fear that I can't trust people hasn't let me do that. So I was nervous about saying how I felt, but I decided I was up for the challenge.

First I started by trying to tell her all I thought and felt, the good as well as the bad. Then I started trying to express the emotions I would rather not expose, like telling her when I miss her. She responds like any typical female. She says stuff like, "That was so cute."

I have kept my feelings bottled up since I was 10, the year two of my best friends died.

But even though I'm getting more comfortable telling her what I think and feel, expressing those emotions I don't feel like talking about isn't getting easier. Sometimes my girlfriend won't realize how hard it is for me, and she will change the subject or even start singing or acting stupid when I'm about to say something I really need to say. That's when I think, "Either I'm boring her or she don't want to hear it." Then I stop talking and don't say anything more until she asks me to. It takes a lot of trust to expose my innermost thoughts and feelings. It can be frightening to trust her, because if she breaks my trust I will feel worse.

Now that we are getting deeper into the relationship, my feelings are growing more. We talk every night. No matter the time, we always make sure we put one another to sleep. But at the same time, I am still taking my time with showing her my feelings, because we both don't want to rush into something we are not ready for.

As I am growing older and more mature, I don't find the same things fun anymore. The idea of playing a female intentionally just doesn't sound fun. What sounds better is trying to build a good relationship by working to trust and be trustworthy, and showing my feelings more. I am respecting females a little more, and I'm feeling the benefits of it.

Antwaun was 18 when he wrote this story.

Reaching Out to My Enemy

By Chantel Clark

In my senior year of high school, Kim was my worst enemy. She had a carefree attitude, not caring what people thought or said, and dressed how she wanted regardless of trends. She was dark-skinned, with short hair she often wore in braided extensions. Every month she mixed in a different color—blue, red, neon pink.

And Kim was loud for no damn reason. I think she just liked to hear herself talk. She was quick to curse people out. She'd get nasty with you in a heartbeat. She was rude, but she was also very intelligent, a secret I figured out when I had math with her and was amazed that this "ghetto fabulous" girl was so smart.

I was a trendsetter, following my own dress code, just not to the same extremes as Kim. I looked like I was going somewhere exclusive every time I came to school. My friends joked that I was going to the clubs every day, because I wore makeup and dressed up 95% of the time. Plus, I was in hair school on the side, so you know a sister was sporting every hairstyle created by man. I was a real vain person on the outside, but inside I was constantly trying to understand who I was.

Kim and I had different styles, but we were a lot alike, and we found each other threatening because of that. In freshman year we got in a fight. She started it, over some he-said, she-said. I wanted to avoid it, but people were all around and I couldn't chump up. I won, and I gained my respect.

> **We were a lot alike, and we found each other threatening because of that.**

After that, I had to live up to my reputation. So when I walked past her, I had nothing to say. Plus, people hype you up, and they added to our rivalry, saying things like, "That's why Chantel won," or "Chantel got like Tyson on her."

After that, Kim and I constantly bumped heads. If we saw each other in the mall, we would roll our eyes at each other. If we saw each other at a party, we made it our business to walk past each other with disgust.

But when I came back to school from summer vacation senior year, I saw my archenemy and she was no longer the same. She seemed to have fallen apart. She didn't do her hair or dress nice anymore. She didn't even hang out with her group of friends. Normally, this would be bait, a perfect opportunity to make her feel down and out. And I began to see people picking on her for no reason, calling her names, throwing things at her, and starting fights.

Her face wore more pain than a woman in labor, her eyes held a sadness that was undefined. I heard through people that Kim was homeless. In fact, I heard her mom kicked her out for a man, and forced her to live in a shed in the backyard. I heard she barely ate, and I saw she was getting skinny. Her face looked like death and, honestly, I was worried.

For the first time, I actually did not want to pick an argument with her. I knew the pain she wore—that face was a face I had hidden inside. And now it was staring back at me like a reflection in my mirror.

I know pain first hand, and it's weird—once you've been hurt or gone through some trials, it's like you know when someone else is hurting inside. You can sense it, you can feel it. I had a yearning inside to talk to Kim, because I was sure I could speak to her like no one else could.

You see, my mom chose men over me, so I know the feeling. And my aunt did the same thing to my cousin. I come from a family of broken women and misleading men, so I understood her pain.

One day I went to see Ms. Bee, a social worker in my school. In her office I saw Kim crying. I felt a heaviness in my chest. I wanted to reach out to her, but I couldn't.

God forbid if I tried to talk to her. What would people think? I also thought to myself, "What if I'm trying to be nice and this chick gets smart? I might curse her out." So my pride, temper, and attitude kept me still.

I left Ms. Bee's office wondering what I could do. How could I speak to her? What would she say?

I returned to Ms. Bee's office later that day and asked her what was wrong with Kim, but she knew our rivalry and said it was confidential. So I asked Ms. Bee if she could set up a meeting between me and Kim. I explained that I saw how much pain she was in and wanted to help in any way I could.

Ms. Bee was shocked, but she knew my life story and that I would be able to say things to Kim that only the two of us could have understood.

About a week or so later, Ms. Bee called me into her office and Kim was there. I suddenly felt out of place and weird, but I went in anyway.

I said to Kim, "I came from a broken home, my life was never a bowl of cherries. My mother, a drug abuser. My father, missing in action. No one knew when he would pop up. My family has more stories than an old Negro testimonial, but I was strong enough to overcome." I told her, "You're beautiful and strong, and if you ever need a shoulder to cry on, I'm here."

Kim was shocked, looking at me with this face that said, "No way." I guess she never saw me as the type to have a hard life, because I hide it so well. So I had to say, "Yes, it's true."

After that, we listened to each other's stories and became friends so quick. We shared similar lives, and we built a friendship out of past hurt and pain.

> *I knew the pain she wore—that face was a face I had hidden inside.*

Kim told me about her mom and how it felt to be forced to live in a shed. She told me that her mom took away all her clothes that she'd worked hard to buy and gave them to her sisters. So now she was stealing to survive.

I told her about my drug-abusing mother and my good-for-nothing father. How at age 5 I almost died because my uncle got high and started a fire. I told her that my dad slept with my aunt, my aunt's daughter, and eventually tried to sleep with me. I told her about my brother, who is a woman-beater, and my sister, who is HIV-positive.

I told her how this fairy princess in a glass castle is my image, but it's only a lie. We told each other things that almost nobody knew, and we laughed about it, too. It's crazy, but I do find my life funny—how could you not? And laughing about it helps me get through it.

After that conversation we became true friends, because we trusted each other. People often stared at us and talked behind our backs, because we were once enemies, now friends. They could never understand the relationship we had.

Kim needed me as her support system, her friend. I made it my duty to give her what she needed. I gave her clothes, lent her money, and snuck her in my house to eat and to hang out. We became like sisters.

By showing who we really were, we realized we could both change, be ourselves. She recognized that her pink braids were for getting attention. She didn't need to be loud and vulgar to be respected. Before she acted like she had a real attitude problem, but that was just a front. So she changed.

She also stopped blaming herself for the way her mother treated her and for the way she had to live. We talked a lot about living life to the fullest, despite the cards God dealt us. And she began to feel determined to survive what her mom was putting her through. Eventually I saw Kim acting like her old self again, the girl who I could talk bull to, and she would come right back with a remark.

Kim gave me emotional support as well, even about little things. I found out I didn't need to wear a lot of makeup to be me. I was just as pretty without it. More than that, though, I found out that I didn't have to pretend all the time, that I could be me without worrying about what anyone else would think.

Kim and I realized we could be honest with each other. We both really needed one real person in our lives—someone who didn't care if your feelings got hurt or if you got mad, as long as she told you the truth.

I helped Kim to find herself again. And in return, I found me.

Chantel was 21 when she wrote this story.

Riona Faith O'Malley

Want a Friend? Be a Friend!

By Antwaun Garcia

Foster youth often feel like outcasts, reluctant to trust others. This can make it difficult to make and keep friends. I interviewed Mary Stephenson, co-founder of Chrysalis Center for Family Development in Kansas City, Missouri, about how youth in foster care can make meaningful connections and keep up good relationships.

Q: Do youth in care have more problems making friends than other people? If so, how come?

A: Of course! It is a combination of not having trust in people and fear of rejection.

Many foster youth come from homes where they were neglected or abused. These early experiences lead them to believe, "My mom rejected me, so who else would want me?"

If a child couldn't trust their parents and caregivers to meet their needs when they were young, they grow up to fear that people who may have no intention of hurting them will also reject or betray them.

Youth who are moved frequently from home to home or were only placed in group homes are most likely to have difficulties making good friends. That's because they never got to practice keeping long-term relationships. It's hard for them to trust people because they always wonder, "Are they actually going to be there? When are they going to walk out?"

Q: Why is it important to have friends? Why can't we just have associates?

A: Human beings need friends for emotional intimacy. You need people with whom you can express your emotions and share dreams, hopes, and fears—things you wouldn't share with an "associate." Friends provide good support for each other when things are rough, help each other make good choices, and really make us feel better about ourselves. Friends help us to better understand ourselves and other people.

Q: What makes a good friend?

A: Some of the qualities of a good friend are loyalty (someone reliable you can count on), trust (fulfilling promises and following through on plans), honesty (no lies), and being realistic (they're upfront about what you can expect from them).

Q: What should we do when a friend disappoints us or hurts our feelings?

A: It is important to be calm before discussing a problem with a friend. The more emotional we are, the more likely we are to fight. To resolve a conflict with a friend, first you must take responsibility for what you did. Pointing blame back and forth won't resolve anything.

If you have a misunderstanding, be the bigger person and

apologize first. Be willing to open up and to talk about it. Start by getting the facts, stating what you feel, and then listen calmly to what the other person has to say.

If, for example, you heard that a friend had spread a rumor about you, if you just accuse your friend of passing on gossip about you, or not caring about your feelings, she might get really mad at you just because of the strong way you came at her. Things go better if you are calm and treat people the way you would like to be treated.

So wait until you're calm to approach her. Say something like this: "I heard you passed on a rumor that I went out with Junior. Is that true?" If your friend denies doing this, and you don't believe her, you can say, "I hope if you hear anything about me, you would check with me before passing it on."

Joining in some kind of activity can make it much easier to make friends.

If she admits she passed on the rumor, you can say: "I feel betrayed and upset that someone I consider a friend would gossip about me."

Q: How do we know when a friendship isn't good for us?

A: The longer an individual doesn't have a friend, the more desperate they become to make one. That's one reason why some teenagers in care may get involved with the wrong crowd. The friendship isn't good when the other person is smothering or controlling you or pressuring or threatening you to go down a negative path.

Q: How can you make friends if you are shy or find socializing really difficult?

A: Joining in some kind of activity can make it much easier to make friends. Get involved with people who share your interest in something, whether it's a school group, church group, college club, sports, or arts organization. Joining a group makes it easier because you already know you have something in common. From there, start very slow. Begin with casual conversations.

Ask a non-personal question such as, "What did you do this weekend?" or, "Have you seen this movie?" This gives you an opportunity to see if you share a connection and see things similarly. Gradually, you can get a little more personal and ask the person out for coffee or a movie. Then, ask questions that will help you know them better, and let them know something about you.

Antwaun was 20 when he wrote this story.

My Sister and Me

By Cynthia Orbes

When it comes to relationships, my sister Natalie and I are very different

One day I was at my sister's house and she, her girlfriend Asja, and I were just sitting around. Her girlfriend grabbed her and picked her up and asked her, "Do you love me?"

"No, I do not love anyone," Natalie said with a smile on her face.

Then her girlfriend dropped her on the couch. Natalie was saying, "No, come back…"

Her girlfriend said to me, "See, your sister doesn't love me." She seemed a little hurt.

"Natalie," I said, "how could you be so mean?"

For a long time I saw my sister as very cold-hearted because she didn't fall in love with anyone. Me, on the other hand, I fall in love too quickly and try to keep the person in my life no matter what. After they freak out and push me away because I'm so clingy, I become upset. Then I act like I don't care, which usually gets the other person even more involved with me. I know, I'm slick.

So it's hard for my sister and me to understand each other's styles.

Natalie can't understand why I'm usually dating more than one guy at a time. It's not because I don't want to commit to someone, it's because I'm afraid to. I always want another guy around just in case.

For a few years I was dating a guy I considered the love of my life. After I fell out of love with him, but while we were still together, I started seeing other guys, too. I was telling Natalie that once, and she said, "What the hell, Cynthia! Come on, stay with Ismael. Don't do that."

"But he always threatens to break up with me. I don't think I'm in love with him anymore," I said. "I want someone who is more my type, who is not shy or unconfident."

"All right, then just tell him you want a break and to be with someone else right now."

"No, because he needs me and I don't want to hurt him. And what if I'm wrong? What if I don't find someone else better? So let me just do it like this now and not hurt him by telling him," I pleaded.

I fall in love too quickly and try to keep the person in my life no matter what.

"OK, whatever," Natalie said. She couldn't understand how I could be so afraid to be alone for even a little while.

I don't understand Natalie either. She goes out with people and gets close to them, spending more and more time around them, but she still won't develop intense feelings for them. She says she likes being free and wild, and avoids intimacy.

She wasn't joking when she told Asja she didn't love her. Not long ago Natalie broke up with her.

"What the hell? You're breaking up with Asja? Don't do that to her. Come on, Natalie, you know you love Asja. Would you like it if someone broke your heart?"

"No, but I don't know…" she said.

"Well, you have to find out what you want and stop breaking people's hearts," I told her—which is advice I should take myself.

I understand that Natalie doesn't want to get hurt and I admire that she thinks about herself and her future. But I worry when she says that she just doesn't fall in love, that she never feels like that. She says, "Relationships are luxuries," and "You don't need a partner."

I wonder if she wants to shut herself off to love because she saw how my father treated our mother, and she doesn't want anyone to do the same to her. (He was violent and mean when he was drunk.) But it could just be that she likes being alone, spending time by herself or with friends and having nothing to worry about.

For me, I worry that I need a man too much. I think that I need to feel loved because I never felt loved by my father. I was always afraid of him and he never told me he loved me. But I remember a few tender moments when my dad took care of me. Maybe I don't have the scared feeling that Natalie has because I felt tenderness for a few moments and want it back so badly.

I think the difference in our ages might also affect how my sister and I see love. My sister had more responsibilities because she was older and was treated like an adult. She probably wanted to feel less responsible for others. I got to be a kid, and in my relationships I still look for guys to take care of me. My sister fears that getting close to someone else will get in the way of her future, but I fear that if I don't have anyone by my side to help me then it will be harder to reach my goals.

Both of our parents died when we were still young—I was 8 and Natalie was 10 when my dad died, and two years later our mom died. Their deaths gave me a fear of losing someone once

I loved them. My strategy is to love and then try to prevent the loss. Natalie's is not to love at all.

But my way of getting close too quick is risky. My mind feels like it's in love with someone I don't even know very well, and who doesn't know me. Just knowing that I connect with someone excites me. It feels good but it's not real love. It's just pretending.

Natalie and I would probably both be better off if we could be more like each other. I think she'd be happy if she really trusted someone enough to fall in love. And I'm trying her method of not falling in love that easily. I have a new boyfriend now, and I'm holding back my feelings a little bit. I say to myself, "Do not even fall in love with him. Wait and see if you still want to be with him in the future."

It's hard, though. At the beginning of our relationship things were up and down, and he told me he wanted to wait

I need to feel loved because I never felt loved by my father.

a month and just be friends, to get to know me before committing to a relationship. I was mad! I wanted to know right away whether he was going to go out with me or not.

"If I'm special, then why wait?" I said.

"If you're special, then why rush?" he replied.

I was outraged at first. Then his words made me feel a little more secure.

We did start dating, and I'm still working on taking it slow. Instead of always thinking of him, I try to focus a little bit more than usual on myself and things that I have to do, like finishing school and getting a job. My boyfriend can't be my whole life.

I hope I can be more like my sister—strong and sure that she doesn't need someone to be there to support her or tie her down.

I also hope she can learn a little from me. When my sister tells me she doesn't need anyone but herself, I just think that is absurd. I like shopping by myself, but that doesn't mean it wouldn't be fun to have someone along to talk to sometimes. There's no reason for her to be so cold-hearted.

I hope that as we get older, I can have more confidence and just stay with one person. I hope that Natalie can also stay with someone and develop strong feelings. Neither of us has ever trusted anyone enough to get close and stay close yet, but I hope we can both find ways to a truly close and trusting deep love.

Cynthia was 20 and attending college when she wrote this story.

Loving and Losing

By Anonymous

The start of my first year in junior high school: new school, new people. I wasn't exactly the guy who shook hands and tried to make friends. I was depressed because my mother had recently broken my heart again. She had told me I would be able to go home before school started, and there I was, still in care. I was the guy in the back of the classroom watching everyone else have fun. I had low self-esteem and I felt that everything was wrong with me.

The only person I could relate to was my cousin Brian. He was also in care and struggling, but the way he handled his situation was by smoking weed. I'd started smoking with him when I was about 11. That's how I dealt with my depression about being away from my family. In school, I just kept to myself and did my work.

One day our class was watching a movie in which the main character's life seemed perfect. I looked down at the ground and said to myself, "If only my life were that perfect." Then I heard a soft voice say, "Tell me about it."

It was the girl next to me. Her hair was curly and her eyes were a seductive hazel. She was beautiful. She asked me why I said that, but I didn't answer. She told me that it was OK to trust her, but my trust wasn't easy to gain.

At lunch the next period, I sat at my usual spot, alone by the window in the back of the cafeteria. I was sticking my fork into my mash-volcano when I felt the table shift slightly. I looked up and saw the same girl from class. "Uh-oh," I thought, "attempt number two."

> **I had never known anyone who would sit there and listen except my therapist, and she was getting paid to do it.**

I was nervous about talking to a pretty girl. My heart was beating like a wild drum, and when she sat down it stopped and hit the floor. I opened my mouth, trying to form a sentence, but nothing came out. Then the bell rang.

Finally, in the hallway, she pulled me aside and said, "Hi my name is Katy Rodriguez."

I stuttered and finally said, "My name is Angel." She seemed relieved to hear me say something.

The next day I saw Katy in the lunchroom. I approached her and I was the one who said hi first. She looked surprised, but then she smiled and we walked to my table. We sat next to each other and talked about the things that 6th graders talk about: music, school gossip, TV shows, etc. From then on we ate lunch together every day.

One day she started to tell me about her life. Her father left her at birth, and her mother was controlling and abusive. She told me that sometimes she would cut herself, but not in places people would easily notice. "If people knew that I cut myself, they would think I'm crazy," she said. "They just don't understand." Her eyes filled with tears.

I looked at her and said, "It's OK. I understand where you're coming from." I said this because I did know, because I'd done that too, and I felt the same way she did about telling anyone about it.

I guess she felt better when she knew there was someone she could connect with, and I felt the same way. When you know you're not the only one, you get this shared feeling of security. In the 45 minutes that she had been talking I felt like I knew everything about her. For the first time in a while, I knew I had a friend.

That day at lunch, I decided I was going to tell Katy about my life. I never talked to anyone about my situation because I knew what they would think. I knew that to other people, being in foster care was like having a contagious disease; they wouldn't want to be next to me. I would have been made fun of and laughed at. But Katy felt different. She had confided in me, and it was my turn to do the same.

I was already at the table when she came and sat next to me. I said, "Katy, I think it's time I told you about my life." She looked happy. I guess she knew how hard it was for me because I kept taking long pauses, but she was patient.

I had never known anyone who would sit there and listen except my therapist, and she was getting paid to do it. I told Katy about being in care, my family, my mom, my reasons for depression, cutting school, cutting myself and using drugs. When I was done, she looked at me and said, "Wow, the impression you give people is way different from what really goes on in your life."

"Yeah, I know," I replied. My eyes were watery, and she hugged me. I felt loved, and so relieved that I was able to express myself, and that she knew what it was like. A huge burden was lifted off my back that day.

Just the Two of Us

One afternoon in June, a few months after we met, I asked Katy out. She said yes and it was the happiest moment in my life. I walked her to the bus stop and we held hands. Then she looked at me, smiled and kissed me. It wasn't the peck on the cheek I was expecting; it was my first real kiss. That day I went home with a smile on my face. I felt like I had died and gone to heaven.

The school year ended so I had to wait another long, stuck-in-the-house summer to see my beautiful baby. Katy was at camp, so I couldn't see her or talk to her. But the good part was I spent most of my time at my sister's house.

To wake up in the same house as my family brought back good memories and made me think about how much I missed them. At any point in the day, from a.m. to p.m., we were always laughing and having a good time. The worst part was leaving.

Seventh grade started off OK. I knew some people who said hi to me when they saw me, and I was happy to be with Katy again. But I was really angry that summer had ended and that once again I was limited to seeing my siblings every weekend. I got even more depressed when my mom told me I'd be going home to her in October, and then it never happened.

During the summer my smoking habit had died down a little, but now that the stress and bad feelings were back, I started up again, and it quickly became a problem.

I was smoking at least three times a day and skipping my afterschool program. Whenever I started to feel bad about what I was doing, I'd already have another blunt in my hand, washing away the thought as if it had never occurred. I came into school high one day. Katy knew what was going on, and she said she had to talk to me.

At lunch, she dragged me to the staircase and said, "What the f--k do you think you're doing? You can't come to school high."

"Well, maybe I needed to get away from the world," I replied.

"And you do that by smoking weed, right? Why don't you get involved in something and stop using little kid excuses."

I stood shut. I knew she was right. We stood there until a teacher came through the door and told us to go to the lunchroom. Katy looked me in the face and said, "I'm disgusted with you, Angel." Then she walked away.

I understood why she was mad. I'd messed up and I was sorry. But for the rest of the day, whenever I tried to talk to her she'd say, "Are you still high?"

I decided that I needed to stop smoking if I wanted to keep my girl. I asked her the next day to help me stop smoking. She said, "Maybe you should get involved in sports?" So I joined the school basketball team. It got my mind partly off of the drugs, but the craving was always there.

I often found myself around my cousin, and when he would look at me and pass the blunt, it was always tempting, but I'd refuse and he always got tight. It was hard because I felt like he only wanted me to hang with him to smoke, and he was supposed to be family. Soon after I stopped smoking, our relationship dissolved.

Luckily, I still had Katy. Our relationship was on a very high level. She even came along on an unsupervised visit I had with my mom, and my mom loved her. I also went over to her house sometimes and had dinner with her family.

We chilled after school almost every day. On most weekends, we would go to the movies or the park, or find a place to hang out and spend the entire day together. At the end of the day, I would walk her home and think about the next day I'd get to spend with her.

Katy and I were at a stage where we could finish each other's sentences and we always knew if the other person was lying about something. She knew my thoughts exactly, and when I was upset she'd tell me to think of ponies and rainbows. It was a little funny actually.

I knew she was right and I couldn't say, "You don't know what I'm going through," because she did know. This bond that had grown between us felt impenetrable; it was something I'd never had before except with my family.

When basketball season ended I once again needed something to occupy my time besides Katy. My mind went straight to my old ways, and she knew, so she had me call her almost every hour to make sure I wasn't high. I was on lockdown, and it worked. I knew if I wanted to stay with my baby I had to control myself. Whenever I felt depressed, I would think about Katy and write poetry.

Toward the end of 8th grade, Katy told me she was moving to Florida, and we had to break up. I cried a lot, because I was losing the best thing that had ever happened to me. I felt like I'd never see her again.

I told her how I felt, and we scheduled a day to meet at our old junior high school. April 8, 2017. We swore to each other that we would meet on this date, and I know I will be there. Hopefully she will be too.

Once we were able to trust one another, the trust we could give to other people grew.

Katy cracked my anti-social shell and opened me up to an unseen world. Once we were able to trust one another, the trust we could give to other people grew. She helped me with my drug issue, and I helped her out at home. One day she told me, "I felt like I was blind from birth, and then one day, I was able to see the world for the first time."

It's been a year now since she moved, and these days I reach out to other people a lot more. I can make friends by just being myself. It's easier to talk to people and tell them about my life now because I realize they might be going through something similar.

I can give them some advice, or I can listen to pieces of their lives and they can share their knowledge. Or maybe I can just let them in on what it's like to be in foster care. When I tell people I'm in care it's funny to see their jaws drop in surprise.

When Katy left, it was hard for me. I still talk to her. We tell each other how much we miss each other, and that we can't wait to see each other again. We bring up old memories and reminisce. I do miss her a lot, but I really can't do anything except hope that time passes by as quickly as possible.

I often find myself feeling depressed, but there's no cure for that. Katy was the person who made my life seem a little better. When my day sucked, looking at her filled me up with joy. She was the only person there to listen and care. She is the girl I loved, and lost.

The author wrote this story when he was 15.

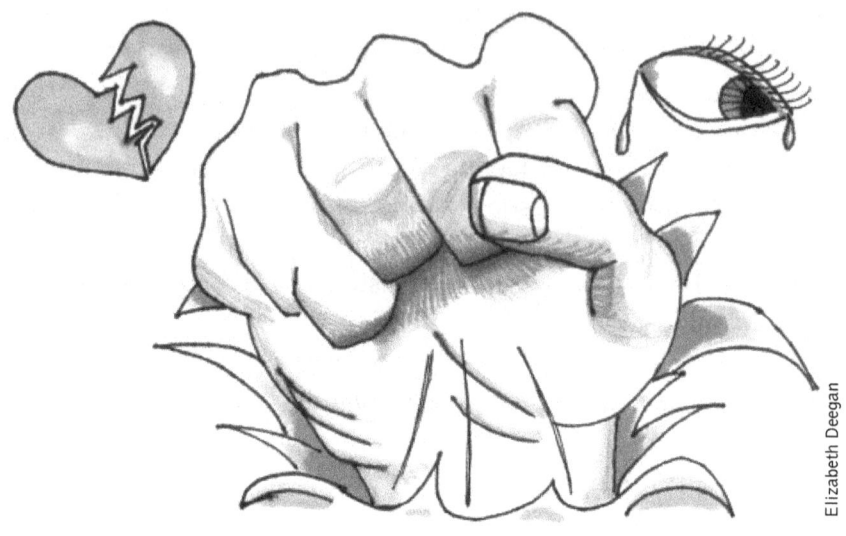

Black and Blue

By Zoraida Medina

As I walk up the stairs, I realize what time it is. Early morning. I've just been with Tony, my boyfriend of one month, who my moms doesn't like. She doesn't like him because he's 19 years old and I'm only 12. I'm hoping she won't do anything, but as I get in front of the door, I feel scared.

I knock.

She asks, "Who?"

I say, "It's Sori."

She opens the door. I see the pain in her eyes. She asks, "Where were you at?"

I say, "With my friends." We both know I've really been with my boyfriend.

She says, "Do you realize what time it is?"

"Yes. It's 5 o'clock."
"You know what's gonna happen, right?"
I say, "Yes." I know from the look on her face.

So she tells me to come in and she hits me and keeps on hitting. And as she's hitting we exchange words. Calling each other names. And it's all of a sudden that I feel she shouldn't put her hands on me, and I tell her I'm going to leave. And I mean it. What I don't know is that the person I'm going to leave her for is going to treat me worse, much worse. But that's how it all begins.

For the next three years I was in my mom's house only off and on. I was with Tony the other half of the time. While my moms only hit me to punish me, like when I stayed out all night, Tony hit me whenever he felt the need. Whenever he was mad he struck me.

When I first saw Tony, he flaunted money in my face and that attracted me. I was coming from the pool with my little brother. I heard someone say, "Shorty." I looked back because people call me "Sori," and that's what I thought I heard. When I looked at him, he already had the money in his hand, knowing that money attracts little girls. It worked. I saw money, and I saw it to be sweet as candy. That was all I needed to see, and it started from there.

The more my mother told me not to be with him, the more time I spent with him.

From the very beginning, my mother didn't want me with him. She thought I was too young to have a boyfriend and he was too old, but I didn't listen. He was my first boyfriend and I considered myself very grown and bold to be with him, so the more my mother told me not to be with him, the more time I spent with him, even after he started hitting me.

One day I wanted to go to a party and Tony said that I couldn't. I looked at him and said, "Are you bugging?" So he slapped me. That was the first time I stayed out all night with him. I did it just because he told me to. I was kind of worried about how my mother would react with me being gone so long, but I was more worried about what would happen if I said no to Tony.

Over a year went by and things just got worse. I was still with him, living with him now. I was a 14-year-old in a relationship with a 21-year-old. I missed my mother every day that we were away from each other. I needed her, and she was still trying to get me out of the relationship, but now I felt I had no other choice than to stay with Tony. If he hit me for no reason when I was with him, imagine what would happen if I left him. I knew I might end up dead or in a hospital. I didn't want to think about it. And it wasn't just fear that kept me with him—all his hitting and insults made me feel bad about myself, like I couldn't get anyone better than him.

Another year went by. I was going on 15. I stopped going to school because Tony would show up there to harass me. Kept going through it all: beatings, insults, arguments, stress. I got punched, kicked, slapped, slammed against walls, floors, mirrors. He used to call me names, everything he could think of.

We argued for the most stupid reasons, like if I didn't cook or clean. If I came home 20 minutes late he would slap me and then we'd argue. Stress, stress, oh God. And I was tired, so tired. Tired of getting hit. Tired of living the life of someone's slave. Tired of getting followed, of being embarrassed, of being treated like I didn't deserve to set foot on the ground. Tired of smoking weed and cigarettes just to calm myself down.

I truly hated Tony by this point, but I also felt stuck with him. So I learned how to act in ways that wouldn't upset him as much. I acted as if I had no friends, as if the world I was living in was over, and the more I acted like this, the more I started believing it. I felt so ashamed all the time. My relationship with my family was nothing but a whole bunch of regrets.

Tony hit me so bad one day outside, and thank God the cops were there to stop it, 'cause I could've been killed. Then the cops gave me advice. They told me to get an order of protection on Tony so he couldn't come near me.

Having them tell me to do that helped, because I kept thinking about what they said. The following week I did get the order of protection against Tony.

I had been in and out of my mother's house, running away and coming back for some time. Now I went back to her house for good. My mother was happy about that. She got a lawyer and helped me make my case to him so that the beatings and pain could stop forever.

The day before my 16th birthday, I was with my uncle and aunt when we spotted Tony. He was coming toward me and I told myself I was going to stop running from him. He came to my face talking crap. He said he had a gun, and if I wasn't gonna walk with him he would start shooting. Little did he know that my uncle had gone to call the cops. The cops caught Tony and searched him. They asked me if this was the man I had the order of protection out on. I said, "Yes." They set me a court date for the next day—my birthday.

> *I was young and confused and I didn't think before jumping into a relationship.*

As I walked into the courthouse, Tony walked in, too. I started crying, I was so scared. Tony had ruled my life for the last several years, all the time I'd been growing up. I'd wanted to kill him so many times and now I was going to testify against him in front of people. I was more than willing to spend my whole birthday in the court because I needed to find my way out of those dark clouds and into the sun where I knew I belonged.

The day I turned 16 years old, at 5 p.m., they found Tony guilty of statutory rape, endangering a minor, and drug abuse. I got him locked up.

I felt free from the cages in my mind. I knew I wasn't stuck

Just the Two of Us

anymore in a world of hate, lust, and fear. I could finally go back to being myself, alone with my family.

But just because Tony's locked up doesn't mean the pain is over. I'm still scared of him getting out of jail and hurting me. At night I have dreams of him trying to kill me, strangle me, run me over with motorcycles. I'm scared to be alone, without anyone to hold or comfort me. To this day, I jump at any unexpected touch or noise.

It hurts to look back on all those years I was with Tony, that period of pain and anger, of having the desire to kill the man who hurt me every day, of having barely any communication with my mother. I was young and confused and I didn't think before jumping into a relationship. I was 12 going on 13, and didn't know what was good and bad for me, and before I knew it I was stuck. I'm glad, so glad, that I'm not stuck anymore. I still hurt from it, but at least that time is over.

Zoraida was 18 when she wrote this story.

Terrence Taylor

How to Know if a Relationship Is Good for You

It can be tempting to jump from a bad relationship to a new one that seems better. But how do you know whether to trust a new person? What does a balanced relationship look like? Dr. Karyl McBride is a psychotherapist specializing in treating children who have been abused. She spoke to us about healthy relationships.

Q: What makes a relationship healthy?

A: When you are connecting with someone who brings out the best in you and the relationship is not based on "What can you do for me?" Both people share ideas, feelings, respect. Both people listen and talk, and they do things to help each other.

Empathy, really trying to feel what the other person feels, is a huge piece of a healthy relationship. It's not trying to fix their problem, but just listening to them.

Often adults tell young people what they should be feeling or how to fix the problem. Everybody, including teens, needs someone to hear what they are feeling, because it helps us figure it out. We make better decisions when we know what we are feeling.

In a healthy relationship, you can be your real self. You don't have to act like somebody else to be loved or accepted.

Q: How do you find your real self?

A: By thinking and talking about your own feelings. If you act from your own feelings, you'll be true to your own values. You're not worrying about what other people want you to be or what the media tells you to be.

Q: What questions should you ask yourself about a new relationship?

A: Here are a few:

Is the person able to give and take?

Do you feel valued for who you are rather than what you can do for them?

Can you be yourself?

Can the other person?

Can you have boundaries? Do they respect them? Can you say "I can't talk now, I have to do my homework," or, "I'm not comfortable telling you that yet"? Or, "I don't want to have sex yet"? You deserve your own space: intellectual space, sexual space, actual physical space, emotional space. And stick to it! Boundaries only work when we enforce them and follow through.

Q: If you've been abused, how do you know who to trust?

A: The first thing to realize is that you are going to have trust issues, and you're probably going to have them forever. You need to recognize that.

Take it slow with people you don't know. Give them a chance to prove to you that they can be trusted. Don't tell them your whole life story the first time you meet them. You can have boundaries around the pain in your life and you get to choose who you share it with.

The more that you learn to trust yourself, the more comfortable you will be in trusting others because your boundaries protect you from people who make you uncomfortable. If we're listening to our inner voice, we will pick up the red flags of another abuser or any other danger.

Q: How can you get help to begin healing and work toward healthy relationships in the future?

A: Getting treatment is very important, because abuse can have long-term effects on your other relationships, including repeating the cycle (being abused again and/or becoming abusive yourself). There are a lot of places that provide therapy for free or at a reduced rate.

Because therapy is so important for working through trauma, ask, ask, ask, until you find the resources you need.

For Love or Money

By Erica Harrigan

I met A-Jay through an ex-friend of mine. My first impression was, "Ugly," but he carried himself well, so I didn't care too much about his looks. We were friends before we caught feelings and started dating. He seemed real sweet, but the deeper we dated the more sour he became.

When we first got together, I thought A-Jay and I could be serious, so I decided to open up my heart and give him my all. I didn't want to play pretend like I usually did, keeping a big smile on my face while I felt hurt or angry inside. I wanted him to know and like me for who I was.

I told A-Jay that, growing up, I was beaten by my mother, ignored by my sister, and raped by family friends. When I got older, I never really cared what I was doing to myself. I ran the streets and had unprotected sex. I wasn't happy with my life, so

I didn't care if I was putting myself in harm's way.

Living in foster care, I felt alone. I wanted somebody to care about me. So I became a girl who was willing to do whatever a man wanted. I tried to buy my men. I would throw money, shower them with lots of gifts, and expect love in return. Of course, most of the guys I dated were out to use me. They wanted money and sex, and if they didn't get it, they were gone.

It was emotional for me to tell A-Jay about my past. I figured he would see me as an emotional freak. He did not. He saw me as hardy, a survivor.

For a while, A-Jay was like my medicine. He kept me sane. He introduced me to his family and I spent the night at his sister's crib on Saturdays. He wrote his rhymes while I wrote my poems, or we'd listen to music or watch movies together. A-Jay was kindhearted, though I soon found out he caught a nasty attitude when he didn't have the upper hand.

We went on outings once in a while, to the movies or out to eat, but I always paid. He only paid for one date—a pizza party and drinks with friends. I worried that I was still buying a man like I did in the past.

But A-Jay told me he loved me. Times when I talked down about myself, he told me not to. He'd say, "If you can't even care about yourself, how can you care about me?"

A-Jay encouraged me to go to my therapy appointments, and even came with me once or twice. In therapy, I dealt with the pain of my past. I talked about how I hold my anger in until I'm ready to explode at any moment. Then I snap at the wrong person.

He seemed real sweet, but the deeper we dated the more sour he became.

Many times I took my anger out on A-Jay. Sometimes he didn't do anything to hurt me, but I couldn't seem to take control of my tongue, to keep bogus words from flying out of my mouth. Other times, his actions really did hurt.

Once, on his birthday, I came over to spend time with him,

but he went to a strip club with his boys while I stayed at his house watching television. He came home late and wanted to lie up in bed with me after he'd had some girls all over him. I flipped out and went to sleep in the living room.

Honestly, I should have just left when he chose to spend his birthday without me. But I stayed with A-Jay because I figured that the first year of a relationship is like probation. You have to fight and work things out before things can go smoothly.

But things went sour between A-Jay and me after he lost his job. He needed money, and I offered to help until he got back on his feet. I made sure A-Jay was straight with whatever he needed.

I would throw money, shower them with lots of gifts, and expect love in return

Soon A-Jay was buying himself expensive things with my money. Then he would argue and blame me when I was broke. He didn't even look for work while I took care of his expenses. I started to feel more and more like he was just using me for my income.

I got angry. I told him he was taking advantage of me, and I put him down for being a grown man still living with family and with no job. I'd say, "Dealing drugs is not a job. It's OK temporarily, but for a career? Come on! That's a guaranteed jail cell or a casket."

We also argued because A-Jay was girl crazy. He was always on the phone with girls, and he would look at girls as they passed and pay me no attention.

We got in a big fight about it on my birthday. I wanted to go to dinner and a movie, but he had to babysit his nephew. I canceled the plans and stayed over with him. While I was there he was texting another girl. I got jealous, packed my things, and headed toward the train station.

I knew we needed to break up when I began to get physically abusive. One day we were talking about our plan to move in together. He suggested that we move to Los Angeles. Then I found out his ex-girlfriend lived out there and he still had feelings for her! I thought, "He is setting me up lovely. We'll move out there, he'll cheat on me and I'll pay the bills. No way!"

I yelled and called him all types of names. He got mad and pushed me. I picked up a knife and threatened to stab him. Then, because I feared myself, I started taking my things to leave. When he tried to hold me back, I called the cops. We were both out of control.

Later, when I had time to think, I felt bad that I reacted so crazily, threatening to stab him. But I also felt hurt that, as much as he said he loved me, he didn't show it. His love didn't feel like love to me.

As A-Jay was losing my heart, I started to spend more time with my friend Mike. To date Mike, I had to be done with A-Jay. It was a hard decision, but I felt that staying with A-Jay was a big mistake. A-Jay seemed like he'd found out he could milk me dry so he didn't have to stand on the corner and deal to make a dollar. I didn't want to be a girl who let her man walk all over her.

I broke up with him on Christmas. We had a big argument.

"Get your mind right. Think things over and get back with me," A-Jay said.

"I have a new lover," I told him. When I left his house, I felt terrible. Suddenly it seemed obvious that A-Jay tried to manipulate anyone to get money. I felt ashamed that I'd fallen for his scam.

Still, dating A-Jay changed me in a lot of good ways. A-Jay was an improvement on past boyfriends, because he was caring toward me in some ways and tried to boost me up. In the year we were together, I really tried hard to grow up and begin to control my actions and moods.

I'm hopeful that what I learned from dating A-Jay will make things better with Mike. Mike is a good guy, not the playa type, and he's helping me practice doing for myself instead of everybody else. He tells me, "You give and give. People take but you never receive nothing."

Just the Two of Us

I tell him, "For once, someone is pleasing me. Hooray!"

When I'm dealing with my emotional collapses, Michael listens to my issues and holds me. He knows that I have my moody moments and that I take my issues out on the world, and he doesn't take it personally.

When I scream my lungs out, he waits, and after I have yelled until I can yell no more, speaks his mind. Or he leaves me to myself and returns when I've cooled off. He also tells me that I should write whenever I feel like harming myself or others. It works! Writing takes a lot of steam out of my chest.

I'm learning that someone who loves me should not encourage me to do anything that will hurt me. In the past, friends, family and boyfriends stole my stuff, beat me up, used me and mistreated me, made me feel low, lied on me, and talked behind my back while smiling up in my face. I'm through with that. I hope things with Michael will turn out good for me.

Erica was 19 when she wrote this story.
She and Michael later married and had two children.

Player No More

By Rosheed Wellington

I was a young boy, but I understood the game of love so well. I saw my father play the game and it made me want a part of it. He had many ladies under his thumb and he lived off of them like a parasite. One day when I was 12, my father and I went to an office together. He began to flirt with one of the clerks shamelessly. I watched how she flushed with emotion, how she giggled and blushed.

"That's how you know you have them at your feet," he told me. "When you see them giggle like school girls, you know you're doing it right."

I looked at him with an awkward smile and one eyebrow raised. "I'm in middle school. All I date are school girls!"

He burst into laughter and told me, "You'll understand when you're older."

I just folded my arms and turned away with the smart-alecky reply, "And you'll understand when you're younger."

Although I pretended I wasn't interested in my father's little game, I couldn't help but be awestruck by his performance. Like my father, I looked at romantic love cynically.

Because of all the hurt and hypocrisy I had seen between adults who were supposed to be in love, I saw love as trickery of the mind meant to justify sex, companionship, and marriage. Being a poet, I wrote poetic lines like, "Love is but a game meant to be played at high risk." I truly believed it.

Besides, my father wasn't in my life a lot so the little bit I got from him I wanted to keep. My father treated women like toys, so it was only natural that I would too.

But as for style, I didn't want to get mine from my father or movies I'd seen. Talking gangsta just wasn't me. I was into smooth-talking girls and telling them what I thought they wanted to hear.

So once I started playing the love game at age 12, I did what I could to change the game to fit my own image. I had seen how my father played for his own selfish gratification and didn't care that he hurt the women around him, including my mother, who he'd split with years before.

I, on the other hand, hated hurting people. I played to see joy on the faces of the girls I dated, which gave me joy. I played for the rush I felt knowing I could have that effect.

But given the type of game I was playing, I did more harm than good.

Mainly my relationships ended because I acted really mysterious and distant. Although I gave girls affection, I never opened up to them. I would buy girls jewelry, sometimes even clothes, take them out to the movies, and draw pictures for them. I wasn't trying to "buy affection." I was just making up for not getting emotionally involved.

But all of the things I did for them didn't make them any

closer to me. They knew nothing about me. No one did. That's just the way I was. I kept the whole world away.

You see, I went into the foster care system at age 9. In the system, I never got any love from foster parents, who seemed to pass me around like a hot potato. I felt like a liability and a burden to my foster parents and social workers, only slowing them down. Given the life I was living, it felt like no one really cared about me, so why should I care for or open up to anyone? Being distant was the way I acted to protect myself.

At the time, I was also trying to keep the fact that I was in foster care a secret. It was bad enough I had foster care to deal with. I didn't also need to be ridiculed by other classmates about my situation. Since I was keeping such a big part of myself a secret, it felt easier to keep everything about me in the dark.

My father treated women like toys, so it was only natural that I would too.

Even though getting hurt was what I was trying to avoid by being distant and detached, my relationships always ended with broken hearts. Sometimes I would end it and sometimes she would. Either way, they would end with a lot of crying or yelling, sometimes one of us, sometimes both of us. I couldn't stand the broken hearts.

Still, the love game was the closest thing to love I'd ever felt. I wasn't about to stop playing, because the love game made me feel important when no one else did. Maybe deep down I really yearned for love. But feeling important was enough for me at the time.

Then, around age 15, I had a talk with a girl I was dating, Chanelle. We did just about everything together—go to movies, walk through the park, play video games. She was my best friend and soon more than that. We started dating two months after we met and she seemed different from every other girl I had been in a relationship with. She was kind, smart, innocent yet seductively alluring—the type of girl who would give her heart to the first one who put the moves on her.

One day, a few weeks before she was going to move to another state, she asked to talk to me. I asked her, "What did you want to talk about?"

She said, "I wanted to know if you love me."

"That was random!"

"Just answer it! Do you...love me?"

"Where is this coming from? You're just coming out of the blue with such a deep question."

"Why are you avoiding it? Just answer me. Do you love me?

Many guys would have been quick to tell the girl, "Yeah I love you." I know my father would have. But I wouldn't allow myself to lie about something that had so much power to hurt, although it wouldn't be much different from creating the illusion of love like I normally did. I felt that I'd already gone far enough.

I told her, "I can't answer that. You wouldn't like the answer." (That alone kind of answered her question.) Unlike any other girl, she didn't yell at me and break up with me. Instead she put her head on my lap and cried.

I cut myself off from my feelings so much that I got used to it.

"What can I do to make you love me?" she asked. Her eyes filled with tears as she held onto me. Each tear that rolled down her face burned a hole in my soul. I had thought I could have the game without the pain. But Chanelle didn't just make me feel like I mattered in that ego-stroking way I'd felt with other girls. I really did matter to her.

It felt amazing to know that someone loved me. It was also amazingly horrifying to feel good when she was feeling so bad. "How could I be so heartless?" I told myself. "I'm no better than my father."

That "love" conversation we had didn't change how I felt about her. I cared about her as a friend but I just never had that feeling. But it did change my views about love. Chanelle opened my mind and showed me that love exists. For that, I am forever in her debt.

Time went too fast during those few weeks before she left. We didn't talk much but we hung out just as much as usual. We held each other close whenever we were alone.

After she left, I felt broken. I was confused. I now had so many feelings stirring around inside me. Although Chanelle's love had felt wonderful, it also made me feel like the lowest form of trash, for being so heartless to so many girls. I saw how much like my father I really was. All the distrust and hate I had for my father seemed to fall back on me.

I stopped dating for a year. Everything was going to be me and only me. I thought I'd quit the game—and love—for good.

But at age 17 it hit me out of nowhere, and in a matter of months I was head over heels in love with a girl named Ollie. Ever since our first conversation, Ollie has given me a weird butterfly-in-my-stomach-ish feeling, and I get giddy. We talk every night and almost every day. I can say without a doubt I am extremely in love.

From the beginning, the way she apologized for every little thing and seemed so concerned about how I was feeling made me feel protective of her and her vulnerability. I wanted to be her knight in shining armor—I felt obligated to be that for her. Feeling that way let me believe that I could be everything my father wasn't.

Ollie is silly and smart. She's a poet and an artist. Even the way we met wasn't my normal way. I met Ollie on an art website, so the connection wasn't physical and we started off as friends. Given my personality, it wasn't long before I escalated the relationship without even really realizing it.

Since we both draw, one day she asked me, "Would you like to draw online with me?"

"Are you hitting on me?" I asked (even though it was clear

Just the Two of Us

she wasn't).

"Do you want me to?" she replied, and that's how it kicked off. Soon there was some serious flirting involved.

Being with Ollie has caused this weird feeling to move around inside me. Most of my life I felt empty, an emotionless void. I cut myself off from my feelings so much that I got used to it and never realized when I did it.

Ollie somehow brings out those hidden emotions and smacks me over the head with them. It feels good. Even the sad or angry feelings she gives me sometimes don't feel so bad. Before I knew it I was telling her what no other girl or person had ever heard from me.

I tell Ollie I love her every single time we talk. She has become the only important person in my life and I would do anything to make her smile. I want to spend every waking second by her side making her happy.

Sure I'm scared of losing her. But she tells me every day that it's never going to happen and I do the same. I believe we'll never leave each other. I know I'm not perfect and maybe someday I will break her heart, but I want to always be there to repair it. It has been a year since we've gotten together and I haven't had anything to repair yet.

You can say this is a story of "boy meets girl, then falls in love" if you want, but it's not that simple. I didn't learn to trust people or to open my heart and let people in. But I did find the one person I'd been missing all my life. The way I see it, I never let down my guard for a second. She just somehow broke in and colonized my heart.

Rosheed was 19 when he wrote this story

In Search of Myself

By Seandrea Evans

A couple months ago, I met my boyfriend through my foster sister and her husband. They were trying to match him up with someone who wanted a serious relationship and who knew what she wanted to do with her life. In a nutshell, he wanted someone like me.

Like me, my boyfriend is quiet, family-oriented, faithful, and works hard to make his relationships work, which is what I love about him.

But when we're together, I'm often unsure about how to act or what to say. Should I be old-fashioned and serious, or should I act funny, playful and outgoing, like I am with my sisters? Should I express my deepest feelings and fears? Or should I be like my mother—cold, unemotional, and aggressive? I don't know if these different sides are all parts of me, or if they're only mirror images of the people who raised me.

It's also hard to be myself because I've always been afraid of people's reactions. I've never known what it was like to have complete trust in someone. My mother was a very unpredictable woman. You never knew when she was about to blow.

And moving from foster home to foster home, I felt like I had to adapt my personality to each foster mom's liking or she wouldn't put up with me. Instead, she might say, "Forget this, I don't have to put up with your mess," and off to another foster home I'd go.

Molding myself to fit in with each foster mother kept me in a constant state of fear. They could set a limit on what they would put up with, and not knowing exactly what these limits were made me fearful that I would cross them.

Over the years, I began to lose my sense of self. My foster families' ways of thinking and acting became my ways of acting and thinking, and I forgot who I was. Now I change my personality so much that it's almost second nature, like a chameleon always changing color.

I act so many different ways that it's hard to know how I want to respond in certain situations, especially with my boyfriend. When he tells me, "Be yourself," I don't know what that really means.

I've never trusted anyone enough to even try to be myself. But that's no way to live.

I want to feel what it's like to be in love for the first time, and I want my boyfriend to see me and love me for who I am. How can he truly love me if I don't let him know the person I am? And how can I express who I am if I don't even know myself?

Growing up, my relationship with my mother wasn't stable. At times my mother could be the most caring person. Once she tried to make me believe in Santa Claus, and she put a little bit of a white fur coat on a cup, saying it was part of his beard. I thought it was sweet that she wanted to give me hope. Sometimes she talked to me about boys and dance, and told me that I was her beautiful little girl.

But other times she seemed out of control, like she could explode at any moment. If I spoke back or voiced my opinion too loud, or in a tone she didn't like, I had to prepare to feel the wrath of her hand.

Living with my mother, I'd only feel joy for a moment when something good happened. Then came the sadness, anger, pain, frustration, and dissatisfaction. I'd ask myself, "What's wrong with me? Does everyone feel this way?" I felt so alone.

I change my personality so much that it's almost second nature, like a chameleon always changing color.

I was a scared, nervous little girl and I hated school because I was picked on by other children. My mother was very fearful of letting me stray too far from home, so while most children played outside or learned how to ride a bike, I was home with my mother watching soaps, waiting for the monthly welfare check.

When I got old enough to ask why, my mother told me of her visions. I didn't know how to absorb what I heard.

"Visions?" I said.

"I had a vision of you being kidnapped and left for dead in the woods," she told me. I often wondered if she was just being paranoid or if she really had the gift of sight. Either way, growing up with a paranoid mother made me a bit fearful of the world and the people in it. And my mother's inability to control her anger made me unable to express my emotions without fearing that I'd lose all control, like she did.

When I was 12, my mother died of cancer. I lived with my grandmother, then with an aunt. Finally, I went to a foster home. I felt more at ease there than I ever had living with family, and than I ever have since. When I first moved in, I was nervous and quiet. I wanted to be on my best behavior, and I wanted my foster mother to see me as the perfect child.

But outside the house, I changed. I decided I was going to be the exact opposite of the shy and scared little girl I had been. I wanted people to see me as spontaneous, sexy, and free.

At first, I was just trying to be something I was not in order to be liked and popular. But as I grew older, pretending to be flirtatious became a cover-up because I didn't want people to know who I was inside. I believed that if people really knew me, they wouldn't want to be around me. Acting flirtatious allowed me to come out of my shell without having to express the real me and risk getting rejected.

When he tells me, "Be yourself," I don't know what that really means.

Still, I always secretly hoped that the guy I was with was The One. I wanted something stable in my life. I had changed home addresses and schools, and I didn't have any strong relationships with any of my friends. But I didn't find the stability I was looking for, because I picked guys who I couldn't depend on.

One boyfriend was overprotective. At first I thought it was cute than he wanted to be around me 24/7, but later he started to become more aggressive and angry. When I told him I was on punishment for staying out late with him the night before, he smashed his glasses on the ground and stomped on them.

Then I found someone who was funny and friendly. He was easy to talk to and we had a lot of fun together. Unfortunately, he was sexually active and I was not, so after three months we went our separate ways.

During that time, I also found out that acting carefree came at a price. One day my foster mother called me into her room and confronted me about the way I acted with boys. She said other people viewed it as disrespectful and wrong. I felt ashamed and confused that some people had misunderstood the person I pretended to be.

After that, I didn't date for five years. During those years, I moved through four different foster homes, and I didn't feel like I could really trust anyone.

My first foster mother and I started arguing, and I had to leave. I already felt sad about moving. Then my second foster mother made me feel worse.

She'd say, "Why you always wear baggy clothing? What are you trying to hide? Bend your knees when you walk. You walk like a robot. Hold in your stomach, you look like you're pregnant. Stand up straight, you're slouching. Stick out your chest. Don't eat too fast."

I began to wonder, "Is there anything I do right?"

I stood in the mirror counting the many flaws I had and thinking, "How can I lose my stomach?" or, "Am I standing up straight?" Soon I was criticizing everything about myself. My days and nights I spent daydreaming, envying other girl's bodies, wishing I had their looks and popularity.

Comparing myself to others and living in fear of making the wrong move made me feel angry, stressed, and depressed. I would often sit in my room by myself or sleep. I never wanted to go anywhere with my friends, because by the time I dealt with everything I had to go through at home I was too drained to do anything else.

Feeling like I had no one to confide in made me feel alone and isolated. And moving around made me feel even more afraid to trust others. How could I trust someone who would give up on me so easily? When I trust someone I'm putting my emotions on the line, and that isn't easy to do when the people who claim to care about you are constantly hurting you.

Finally, I moved to a home that's not perfect, but where I do feel a lot safer. My foster sister makes me feel so relaxed. She is outspoken and honest about her feelings and non-judgmental when she listens to what I have to say. That makes me want to be more open with her about thoughts and feelings.

When I tell her about my life before I came into care, I tell my story in detail, explaining how I felt in each situation, and it feels like my sister is reading my mind. She knows what I'm about to say before I say it, or she'll give me examples of similar situations she's been through. She is like a diary where I can express what I really think and feel. That's a big relief to me.

My sister also shows me what a trusting relationship can be like. When she's around her husband, she seems so relaxed and true to herself. Even though they argue at times, they also share in each other's lives and they understand one another like best friends. That's the way I want to be with my boyfriend. I would feel relaxed if I had that kind of relationship.

But I don't know what it will take to get to that point with my boyfriend. It's like when you're a little girl and your dream is to become an actress or a rap star—you don't think about the process of getting there, you just imagine yourself there.

My sister says it takes trust, openness, and honesty to make a relationship work. I wonder, "How trusting, open, and honest do I have to be? Should I tell him of my past and my struggles to find my identity?"

I did tell him that my mother used to hurt me. But I never told him what I meant by that and he didn't ask. I wish he would. I wish that he would tell me personal things without me asking him, and that he would ask me personal questions as well.

Other than that, I haven't shared much with him. I'm not that comfortable with him yet and I'm not willing to risk communicating my feelings. I don't want him to think that I'm a nutcase, or worse, pity me.

And often, I don't even know what my feelings are. It's never been safe for me to say how I feel, so many times I can't tell if something makes me happy or sad. I need to start asking myself how I feel, before I can share my feelings with someone else.

My foster mother told me, "Slowly, without even noticing it, you will become closer and closer to him." When I think about all the times we've spent together, it's true that we've become closer. Maybe it's just going to take time for me to get to know myself better, and how I really feel, to become more trusting and open. I hope that someday I will feel more comfortable expressing myself and more confident about who I am.

Seandra attended SUNY-Oswego after graduating from high school.

Stephanie Wilson

My First Friend

By Hattie Rice

If you saw my friend Amanda at the Puerto Rican Day parade, you'd notice her. She'd be loud, wearing a rainbow dress (she loves to represent her color), and pushing people out of the way with an attitude. Her girl Crystal would be trying to get her freak on with her in the street. (Crystal's a freak.) Amanda would be yelling, "What's good, Hattie?"

Amanda has a short temper and is always ready to pop off in a second. When I'm around her I act kind of wild. We'll be on the train just cursing, singing, rapping, and yelling like we 7:30 (a.k.a. nutty). But when we're alone, we can be very serious.

Amanda might be telling me that she wants to run away because foster care gives her the same problems she tried to escape. Other times we'll reminisce about when she tried to teach me how to dance, or when one of my worst fears was realized—when the nuthouse came to get me unexpectedly.

Amanda and I met when I first came into care, and she was the first friend I ever made. When I'm around her I feel comfortable and safe, like no one can hurt me. I also feel like I have someone to depend on, somebody who will be strong when I'm weak.

Before I came into care at age 13, I had become distant from everybody. I never really had friends as a kid, but by the time I got to middle school people never heard my voice. I walked with my head down, trying to hide because I thought strangers were judging me. My paranoia made me so nervous that my hands and legs would shake.

I think I was scared mostly because my mom has schizophrenia, and thinks people are trying to drive her crazy and are looking at her strange. Her ideas rubbed off on me.

My family also said a lot of hurtful things to me, calling me a "fat beast" and "fag" (even though I'm not gay). That really hurt. I felt powerless to object to what my parents said and believed them because I heard them over and over again.

I was teased at school, too. One teacher gave me some positive comments, but many teachers and other kids called me "retarded." I believed them because my mother used heroin and everything else in the book while she was pregnant with me.

Whenever I'm with Amanda I feel OK about being around other people, too, because I trust her so much.

So instead of playing with friends, most of the time I was home playing video games. I got used to not having friends, but I didn't feel good about it.

When I came into my first group home, I was diagnosed as having "social phobia." That means I'm unusually fearful around people.

At that time, I was feeling particularly shy and nervous

because I had no clue what foster care was. All I knew was that I was 13, scared, and lonely, with no family to save me. Separated from my parents I felt all alone, and without my brother I had nobody to talk to. I cried day and night.

The first week I didn't eat or come out of my room. I felt scared to meet the other girls. I thought I wouldn't fit in. Since I'd never had friends, it seemed like me and people weren't compatible.

Locked in my room I thought about my life. The mirror seemed to reflect back to me how unhappy I was. My attitude was always, "If you don't talk to me, then I'm not talking to you." But I knew I needed to start opening up.

Then one day a girl named Krystal came to my room and told me to come down to the recreation room so we could talk. I don't know why I went downstairs. Maybe it was because she looked like a nice person with a warm smile, or maybe I was just tired of being lonely.

Krystal told me she was just like me when she was little and that she felt my pain. She said, "I've been raped and I have more problems than you, but I'm still happy and you should be too."

I could see the pain in her eyes even before she started crying. It meant a lot to me that she even started crying, because that's something a psychiatrist would never do. That helped me start talking to her. Besides, it was difficult to hold my feelings in for all those years. It felt good opening up, like a shadow cast over me was released.

After that I realized that my group home was to my advantage because the girls had had similar experiences to me. Finally I had people to talk to who didn't treat me like I was weird or crazy. I started being more friendly and listening to other people's problems, and developed a more positive outlook on life.

I found that I liked listening to friends' problems. Hearing somebody else's life story satisfies my taste buds. Their life becomes a little escape from my own reality, which is sour.

Not long after I went into care, Amanda became my new roommate. To become her friend, I had to pass a series of tests. If she tells you something and you snitch or don't stand by her side, you fail. I passed with flying colors.

Over time I told her my life story and she told me hers. It touched my heart that she trusted me when she usually doesn't trust anybody. We cried together and everything. It felt good to get close to her. I finally had somebody other than my brother to confide in.

Amanda and I also gave each other solutions to our problems. If staff got on her nerves, I'd tell her, "Just ignore them." She taught me how to stick up for myself and not to flip out on my mother when I'm angry. From her, I learned that I'm intelligent and beautiful, but confused.

The group home staff even started calling her my mother, because she'd teach me cooking, cleaning, and how to maintain myself when I was stressed out. In school, she'd sometimes walk me to class to make sure I didn't cut. Whenever I'm with Amanda I feel OK about being around other people, too, because I trust her so much.

It felt good opening up, like a shadow cast over me was released.

Having Amanda as a friend gives me confidence, but she can't make all my fears just go away. My social phobia still affects my everyday life. When there are more than six people in my group home's living room I leave. I rarely make eye contact. On the train I sometimes shake or feel like I'm being watched. In school I sit in the back and try to blend in the surroundings so nobody says anything to me.

I want to be a woman with self-confidence, diligence, and integrity. As an adult I want to be successful, not trapped by poverty. That's why I forced myself to go back to school and earn an 85 average. My will power helped me change a little bit.

But I know I need help because I still feel uncomfortable

around most people. I think in order to heal I need to let all my feelings out, but I don't know many people that I can depend on or feel comfortable talking to. Even though deep inside I hardly trust people, I'd like to see a psychiatrist because I don't want to have social phobia forever.

For now I have Amanda's support. It's easy to confide in her, because if I start crying about something, she's usually been through it too. One day I told her how I feel about my mother. I told Amanda that my mom is a crackhead and I had to take care of her emotionally.

In return, Amanda told me that when her mother was alive she was a crackhead too, and would do crack in the corner while Amanda fed her sisters any food she could get her hands on. After that, she and I just cried, feeling each other's pain. It felt good to let it out.

Hattie was 16 when she wrote this story.
She later attended SUNY Binghamton.

Nelle McKay

Playing To Win

By Fred Wagenhauser

I met Katherine one day at the JOY Center, a place where youth from my neighborhood come together and play video games and basketball. Katherine was sexy, played sports and was hood, too. I wanted to holla at her, but I was too shy.

Then Chris, a friend we had in common, got locked up, and Katherine was sad. That's when she and I got closer. We would rollerblade, go to Central Park, play sports, and chill while listening to music. I liked that we had so many common interests. But then she got a job and I didn't see her for a while. It seemed like I would never get a chance to make her my girl.

One night when I was chilling outside the center, Katherine came over and started to talk to me. I was really feeling her. We took a walk with my friend L.S. and everything was good. When I stepped out to use the bathroom, she called her boyfriend and broke up with him.

When I came back, L.S. told me to holla, she's available. I asked her, "You want to try Whiteboy for a trial period?" She did. I was elated. Seeing that she liked me too had me feeling good about myself.

Over the next few months I took her to the movies, bought her things, and had fun with her. I'd never spent money on a female before, but I was treating Katherine like a queen.

One day I told her, "Since the first day we met I was feeling you. I always wanted to talk to you but never had the courage." She sat there all quiet, leaving me to wonder, "Does she feel the same way?"

Despite my strong feelings, I had other females I was messing around with. I never considered breaking it off with the girls because I didn't trust that Katherine could return my feelings. I thought I might need something to fall back on.

Also, I had no confidence in myself. When I was little I was fat and a complete nerd. I was really shy and I loved to read more than anything. In school I was always picked on for my cheap clothes, messy hair, and lack of social skills.

Oh yeah, another good reason I was lacking confidence? For a few years starting when I was 4, my father raped me and told me that I was gay and I would never amount to anything. My own father betrayed my innocence and my trust. How could I trust anyone else?

For a long time after that I just shut down. It wasn't until I was about 16 that I started to attend groups to help me deal with the pain. I'm still working on healing myself.

The anger and shame I felt led me to violence, and I spent most of high school in a residential treatment center and then locked up. When I got out, I was still fat and felt low about myself. It's was hard to see myself as anything but a failure.

But I finally started to lose weight and people began complimenting me on my looks, even telling me I should be a model.

One time I was riding the bus with my friend Nelson. Mad females were looking at me and passing me the eye. Later he started to complain about how when I'm around he gets no play. Comments like that helped bring up my confidence level.

Soon I started to date and I felt good. My next problem was that I was a virgin, since I'd been locked up from age 13 to 18. I was always being made fun of because I hadn't had sex yet.

When I finally lost my virginity, I had the confidence of a million men. I became a man-whore. I'm not trying to brag but I know how to lie. I told females whatever they wanted to hear just to get in their pants. Sometimes it didn't work but most of the time it did.

But I guess I didn't really have the confidence to make a girl my own yet, to really trust that a girl would like me long-term. So I kept it from Katherine that I had other girls on the side.

I didn't really have the confidence to make a girl my own yet, to really trust that a girl would like me long-term.

I knew what I was doing was wrong because I felt guilty around Katherine. It got so bad I couldn't look her in the eyes because I thought that she would see right through me. I stopped bugging her to come to my place because I worried she would bump into one of the other girls.

One night at the JOY Center I heard that Katherine was bad mouthing me and talking how she'd had sex with a friend of mine. I was heated so I told a friend to let her know it was mutual. Somehow, I thought that if we both admitted we'd made mistakes, we could forgive and move on.

But when she heard, Katherine approached me like a mad bull. She said, "You cheated on me and I didn't know!" She raged at me, but instead of feeling compassion, I raged back. "You were too dumb to see all that was going on," I told her.

She pushed me and I went to swing. I wanted to take her head off. I'd never been disrespected by a female like that and didn't know how to handle it. Luckily my friends grabbed me and took me out

L.S. said, "Damn, Whiteboy, I never saw you so heated before. It looked like you had fire in your eyes."

"You would too if a girl was asking to be knocked out!" I told him. I'd never been so embarrassed and angry in my life. I felt like people could see the anger coming out of me.

Later on, I saw Katherine was crying. I didn't expect it because 20 minutes prior she was screaming. That hit a low chord in my heart and I had tears coming down my face. I felt I would have done anything to make her stop crying, but it was too late.

I expected to feel indifferent and uncaring about Katherine. After our fight, I didn't think I'd hurt so much. But I was honestly devastated. The pain was with me all the time, from when I woke up until I went to bed.

I went on a drinking binge for two months. I was so drunk most of the time that I couldn't feel the pain. I also went out and robbed people for money. I really didn't need it, I just wanted to feel a thrill, and I was half hoping to get locked up or killed.

> *I expected to feel indifferent and uncaring about Katherine. But after our fight, I was honestly devastated.*

During that time, I confided in my mom about my drinking and the robberies I committed. She yelled at me for being like my father, because he did the same things when he was young. It hurt like hell but I knew she had a point. She knows I don't want to be anything like my father so it kind of scared me straight.

I felt so guilty, ashamed and overwhelmed. I wanted to right my wrongs and have a clean slate. So I decided to call all of the girls I'd been messing with and explain that they were not the only one.

I called them all and talked to each a little bit, hoping they'd be as relaxed as possible when I told them the bad news. Some yelled at me and that was cool— I expected it. It was the crying that was unbearable. When one girl broke out crying on the phone, I had to hang up on her because that was too much for me. I felt like an evil person. It was a lot for me to shoulder.

Finally I told myself I had to move on, and fast, or I would be spiraling down an endless mess of heartbreak and confusion. I started to join gyms and youth centers that would keep me happy and busy so I wouldn't think about Katherine. It took a few months but I was maintaining and moving on.

Then I met Lizzy. I thought we could have a good relationship. She was a sweet and caring person. But karma got me good.

Lizzy and I started out as friends. I met her through my brother and we would always chill. On the Fourth of July we were cuddling during the fireworks and enjoying each other's company. A few days later we decided to become a couple.

I really liked her because she made me laugh and we had fun together. We bought each other gifts, took each other out to eat, skateboarded together, and in general had a great summer. After a while I felt that I could trust her, and I started to fall in love.

But sitting in the park one day, I noticed how my brother was always around Lizzy and that they were paying more attention to each other than to anything else. A good friend of mine pulled me to the side and asked if Lizzy was my girl or my brother's.

"I'm dating Lizzy, why?" I asked.

"Well it looks like your brother is getting more out of the deal than you."

I sat back and observed until I had seen too much. I left. A few days later, Lizzy was over the house and she tried to hug me. "Get the hell away from me," I told her.

When my brother got home that night he tried to bark on me for treating Lizzy wrong.

"You have no right coming at me and telling me I was wrong," I said. "You were wrong. How could you look at me and lie to me the whole time? Knowing that I was falling for her, you went and violated me!"

My brother didn't deny it, and I went outside so I could cool off. I sat there and thought about how getting caught up in matters of the heart made me feel so hurt. So once again, I made a vow to stay single for a hot minute. I figured if I don't do relationships I can't get hurt. No emotional attachment, no commitment, no worries. All I have to look out for is number one.

But the next four months were a miserable time in my life, not because I was single but because I felt so humiliated by what Lizzy had done to me. Finally, I understood what I'd put girls through.

I also realized that when I get hurt by a female, I feel humiliated the way I did when my father hurt me. To make matters worse, I put myself down, telling myself that I'm worthless and no good. Those are feelings I've been carrying inside—and fighting against—for a long time.

> *I figured if I don't do relationships I can't get hurt.*

Sometimes at night I sit and ask God to forgive me for being so dumb. I have been meaning to ask Katherine for forgiveness but she is a hard person to find. I don't exactly know what I'm going to say to her but when I see her I will. If she can forgive me then I have to be able to forgive Lizzy. I'm cool with that.

These days I have a new wifey in my life and I have a job and my own place. I've never felt better. Things are going differently with my wifey than with any other girl I've dated. Why? Because I won't fully trust her until I feel less scared for my heart. I like her and care for her but my heart is at stake and my heart means a lot to me. Whatever I have to do to keep myself safe, I'll do. I'm tired of being hurt. Karma, leave me alone.

From day to day, I feed her tidbits of information and see how she reacts. If she's cool with what I've told her, it brings my trust up a little bit. For example, I told her I smoked and drank. She said she wasn't into all that and I told her I would chill. My respect and trust for her went up a little bit. I also told her how I don't want to be hurt and I'm not looking to hurt her either. Her response was that she's been hurt too much herself to play around.

Now I feel good about myself and my love life. I still have a long way to go, but I've made a hell of a start in making my life better for me.

Fred was 21 when he wrote this story.

Learning To Love Again

By Shaniqua Sockwell

As a child, I always saw love as a magical force that could draw two people together, and they would be that way forever. I read about love in fairy tales, saw it in movies, and heard it on the radio in songs. But I never experienced it in real life.

I guess you could call me one of those hopeless romantics, because I always believed magical, undying love was possible, even though another part of me got to thinking that this love thing must be some kind of hoax. It seemed so wonderful in fiction, but never in reality. At least not for me.

Unlike a lot of girls around my block, I didn't want to get love from all the wrong people. These girls took love wherever they could find it, mainly from men who were much older than they were, and they would endure getting pregnant and experimenting with drugs. They were so desperate for love they'd go with anyone. I was determined not to go down that road.

I would watch men and women holding hands, kissing, and looking into each other's eyes, sharing special messages that only they could understand. I would wonder, "Why can't I have that? Just for once I'd like to have someone tell me they love me and really mean it."

After a while, I got tired of feeling like I didn't need someone in my life, so I started dating. I soon wished I hadn't.

*I*nstead of taking things slow, I would instantly get caught up in the guy I was dating. Looking back, I realize I mistook like for love, and love for like, so it's no wonder I got hurt so many times.

Because of my parents' lack of affection, I didn't really know the difference between the two. But love is a strong word. It shouldn't be said or used unless you mean it, and Lord knows I've had my fair share of heartache from men who used this word to control me. They all knew my one weakness, that I was in great need. From that, they drew upon their ability to hurt me.

One boyfriend would tell me he cared for me, and said it so sincerely that I almost believed him. But if he cared, why did he sleep with my cousin just because I wouldn't give it up?

I began to wonder why I was in need of love so much.

Another boyfriend said that he liked me a lot, that I was funny and sweet, and I wasn't like most of these other girls out here. But is liking me not telling me that he made two girls pregnant and that he was also cheating on me?

The first guy I fell in love with (or rather became infatuated with) told me he loved me because he could talk to me. We discussed science fiction, art, music, and everything else. When we kissed, I saw fireworks. But is love not calling me, standing me up, and then cursing me all the time?

One guy who told me he loved me said I reminded him of his mother. How sweet, but does being in love mean that you tell my mother that you're breaking up with me before you tell me? And then making some lame excuse about wanting to be just friends, and asking me to wait for him? As if he expects me to stop dating just for him!

After all this, it's no wonder that I became a cold, heartless female. Only a fool would put up with this for as long as I did. I began to dislike men with a passion. I stopped dating because I felt that I had been hurt enough, and being alone was far better than being with someone who made me feel bad.

Instead of looking for a fantasy, I started to put my needs first.

It seemed that I couldn't find a decent man, at least one who didn't want to get me "between the sheets." But, on the other hand, I didn't want to believe that all men are dogs, because I know not all of them are. So what was I supposed to think about men?

I began to wonder why I was in need of love so much, why I was so dependent on having someone to call my own. That was when I realized that I never had someone in my childhood to show me any kind of affection, which is why I didn't receive or look for love the right way.

For years, I didn't really know what the word love meant. I mean, I know what it meant, but I didn't know how to express it, give it, or receive it because I didn't receive it as a child.

My biological mother always had a funny way of showing how much she loved me. The closest kind of affection I ever got from her was, "Yeah, I love your dumb #$%^$, now go do the dishes!!" She didn't know what kind of effect this had on me, even when I did the dishes with tears coursing down my cheeks.

I once heard someone say that the first man you ever fall in love with is your father. But what if you don't know who "father" is? What if all you had was a daddy who did drugs and came in all hours of the night and went around with a bunch of different women who you could never imagine calling "mom?" Would you love Daddy then? My daddy told me he loved me all the time, but, like my mom, he had a funny way of showing it.

By looking at how my parents treated me as a child, I realized I had to love myself and accept myself. I've always had low self-esteem, and I felt bad because I've always been considered "different" from everyone else. (Because of how I dress, how I talk, etc.)

But I've come to see that being different is a good thing, because for one, you aren't following the crowd and two, you're being your own person and not worrying about impressing everyone else.

Basically, I was looking for a loving relationship to replace my missing self-esteem. But I had to realize that another person doesn't give you that self-esteem. You have to feel it inside yourself before you enter a serious relationship.

And although I haven't come completely full circle when it comes to how I think about myself, I can now say that I love myself a lot more than I did a few years ago.

Through talking things out with people and thinking about my past relationships, I discovered exactly what my problem was. I was looking for love not in the wrong places, but in the wrong way.

I was searching for my Nubian prince, my knight in shining armor. A fairy tale man. But we hopeless romantics too often forget that fairy tales should be left where they belong. This is not to say that fantasy men don't serve a purpose. They help you visualize the kind of person you want to be with, the kind of person you like.

But I was attracted to fantasy figures because I didn't have a successful male figure in my childhood. I had no idea of what kind of person I should be attracted to. Maybe I was looking for a father figure and a boyfriend at the same time.

Instead of looking for a fantasy, I started to put my needs first. For example, one of my ex's used to stand me up on dates. I couldn't stand it, but I'd let it slide because I really liked him. But

Just the Two of Us

then I realized that I was ignoring my own feelings. So I looked for someone who wouldn't stand me up.

Today, I am much happier. I have a man who loves me as much as I love him. We see each other often. We write love letters. We talk. And he realizes that I have a working brain, and that I use it.

Most importantly, I've learned to be comfortable with myself—whether I'm in a love relationship or not.

Shaniqua was 17 when she wrote this story.
She majored in English and art history in college.

FICTION SPECIAL

Lost and Found

Darcy Wills winced at the loud rap music coming from her sister's room.
My rhymes were rockin'
MC's were droppin'
People shoutin' and hip-hoppin'
Step to me and you'll be inferior
'Cause I'm your lyrical superior.
Darcy went to Grandma's room. The darkened room smelled of lilac perfume, Grandma's favorite, but since her stroke Grandma did not notice it, or much of anything.
"Bye, Grandma," Darcy whispered from the doorway. "I'm going to school now."
Just then, the music from Jamee's room cut off, and Jamee rushed into the hallway.

The teen characters in the Bluford novels, a fiction series by Townsend Press, struggle with many of the same difficult issues as the writers in this book. Here's the first chapter from *Lost and Found*, by Anne Scraff, the first book in the series. In this novel, high school sophomore Darcy contends with the return of her long-absent father, the troubling behavior of her younger sister Jamee, and the beginning of her first relationship.

"Like she even hears you," Jamee said as she passed Darcy. Just two years younger than Darcy, Jamee was in eighth grade, though she looked older.

"It's still nice to talk to her. Sometimes she understands. You want to pretend she's not here or something?"

"She's not," Jamee said, grabbing her backpack.

"Did you study for your math test?" Darcy asked. Mom was an emergency room nurse who worked rotating shifts. Most of the time, Mom was too tired to pay much attention to the girls' schoolwork. So Darcy tried to keep track of Jamee.

"Mind your own business," Jamee snapped.

"You got two D's on your last report card," Darcy scolded. "You wanna flunk?" Darcy did not want to sound like a nagging parent, but Jamee wasn't doing her best. Maybe she couldn't make A's like Darcy, but she could do better.

Jamee stomped out of the apartment, slamming the door behind her. "Mom's trying to get some rest!" Darcy yelled. "Do you have to be so selfish?" But Jamee was already gone, and the apartment was suddenly quiet.

Darcy loved her sister. Once, they had been good friends. But now all Jamee cared about was her new group of rowdy friends. They leaned on cars outside of school and turned up rap music on their boom boxes until the street seemed to tremble like an earthquake. Jamee had even stopped hanging out with her old friend Alisha Wrobel, something she used to do every weekend.

Darcy went back into the living room, where her mother sat in the recliner sipping coffee. "I'll be home at 2:30, Mom," Darcy said. Mom smiled faintly. She was tired, always tired. And lately she was worried too. The hospital where she worked was cutting staff. It seemed each day fewer people were expected to do more work. It was like trying to climb a mountain that keeps getting taller as you go. Mom was forty-four, but just yesterday she said, "I'm like an old car that's run out of warranty, baby. You know what happens then. Old car is ready for the junk heap. Well, maybe that hospital is gonna tell me one of these days—'Mattie Mae Wills, we don't need you anymore. We can get somebody younger and cheaper.'"

"Mom, you're not old at all," Darcy had said, but they were only words, empty words. They could not erase the dark, weary lines from beneath her mother's eyes.

Darcy headed down the street toward Bluford High School. It was not a terrible neighborhood they lived in; it just was not good. Many front yards were not cared for. Debris—fast food wrappers, plastic bags, old newspapers—blew around and piled against fences and curbs. Darcy hated that. Sometimes she and other kids from school spent Saturday mornings cleaning up, but it seemed a losing battle. Now, as she walked, she tried to focus on small spots of beauty along the way. Mrs. Walker's pink and white roses bobbed proudly in the morning breeze. The Hustons' rock garden was carefully designed around a wooden windmill.

As she neared Bluford, Darcy thought about the science project that her biology teacher, Ms. Reed, was assigning. Darcy was doing hers on tidal pools. She was looking forward to visiting a real tidal pool, taking pictures, and doing research. Today, Ms. Reed would be dividing the students into teams of two. Darcy wanted to be paired with her close friend, Brisana Meeks. They were both excellent students, a cut above most kids at Bluford, Darcy thought.

"Today, we are forming project teams so that each student can gain something valuable from the other," Ms. Reed said as Darcy sat at her desk. Ms. Reed was a tall, stately woman who reminded Darcy of the Statue of Liberty. She would have been a perfect model for the statue if Lady Liberty had been a black woman. She never would have been called pretty, but it was possible she might have been called a handsome woman. "For this assignment, each of you will be working with someone you've never worked with before."

Darcy was worried. If she was not teamed with Brisana,

maybe she would be teamed with some really dumb student who would pull her down. Darcy was a little ashamed of herself for thinking that way. Grandma used to say that all flowers are equal, but different. The simple daisy was just as lovely as the prize rose. But still Darcy did not want to be paired with some weak partner who would lower her grade.

"Darcy Wills will be teamed with Tarah Carson," Ms. Reed announced.

Darcy gasped. Not Tarah! Not that big, chunky girl with the brassy voice who squeezed herself into tight skirts and wore lime green or hot pink satin tops and cheap jewelry. Not Tarah who hung out with Cooper Hodden, that loser who was barely hanging on to his football eligibility. Darcy had heard that Cooper had been left back once or twice and even got his driver's license as a sophomore. Darcy's face felt hot with anger. Why was Ms. Reed doing this?

Hakeem Randall, a handsome, shy boy who sat in the back row, was teamed with the class blabbermouth, LaShawn Appleby. Darcy had a secret crush on Hakeem since freshman year. So far she had only shared this with her diary, never with another living soul.

It was almost as though Ms. Reed was playing some devilish game. Darcy glanced at Tarah, who was smiling broadly. Tarah had an enormous smile, and her teeth contrasted harshly with her dark red lipstick. "Great," Darcy muttered under her breath.

Ms. Reed ord e red the teams to meet so they could begin to plan their projects.

As she sat down by Tarah, Darcy was instantly sickened by a syrupy-sweet odor.

She must have doused herself with cheap perfume this morning, Darcy thought.

"Hey, girl," Tarah said. "Well, don't you look down in the mouth. What's got you lookin' that way?"

It was hard for Darcy to meet new people, especially someone like Tarah, a person Aunt Charlotte would call "low class." These were people who were loud and rude. They drank too much, used drugs, got into fights and ruined the neighborhood. They yelled ugly insults at people, even at their friends. Darcy did not actually know that Tarah did anything like this personally, but she seemed like the type who did.

"I just didn't think you'd be interested in tidal pools," Darcy explained.

Tarah slammed her big hand on the desk, making her gold bracelets jangle like ice cubes in a glass, and laughed. Darcy had never heard a mule bray, but she was sure it made exactly the same sound. Then Tarah leaned close and whispered, "Girl, I don't know a tidal pool from a fool. Ms. Reed stuck us together to mess with our heads, you hear what I'm sayin'?"

"Maybe we could switch to other partners," Darcy said nervously.

A big smile spread slowly over Tarah's face. "Nah, I think I'm gonna enjoy this. You're always sittin' here like a princess collecting your A's. Now you gotta work with a regular person, so you better loosen up, girl!"

Darcy felt as if her teeth were glued to her tongue. She fumbled in her bag for her outline of the project. It all seemed like a horrible joke now. She and Tarah Carson standing knee-deep in the muck of a tidal pool!

"Worms live there, don't they?" Tarah asked, twisting a big gold ring on her chubby finger.

"Yeah, I guess," Darcy replied.

"Big green worms," Tarah continued. "So if you get your feet stuck in the bottom of that old tidal pool, and you can't get out, do the worms crawl up your clothes?"

Darcy ignored the remark. "I'd like for us to go there soon, you know, look around."

"My boyfriend, Cooper, he goes down to the ocean all the time. He can take us. He says he's seen these fiddler crabs. They look like big spiders, and they'll try to bite your toes off. Cooper says so," Tarah said.

"Stop being silly," Darcy shot back. "If you're not even going to be serious . . ."

"You think you're better than me, don't you?" Tarah suddenly growled.

"I never said—" Darcy blurted.

"You don't have to say it, girl. It's in your eyes. You think I'm a low-life and you're something special. Well, I got more friends than you got fingers and toes together. You got no friends, and everybody laughs at you behind your back. Know what the word on you is? Darcy Wills give you the chills."

Just then, the bell rang, and Darcy was glad for the excuse to turn away from Tarah, to hide the hot tears welling in her eyes. She quickly rushed from the classroom, relieved that school was over. Darcy did not think she could bear to sit through another class just now.

Darcy headed down the long street towards home. She did not like Tarah. Maybe it was wrong, but it was true. Still, Tarah's brutal words hurt. Even stupid, awful people might tell you the truth about yourself. And Darcy did not have any real friends, except for Brisana. Maybe the other kids were mocking her behind her back. Darcy was very slender, not as shapely as many of the other girls. She remembered the time when Cooper Hodden was hanging in front of the deli with his friends, and he yelled as Darcy went by, "Hey, is that really a female there? Sure don't look like it. Looks more like an old broomstick with hair." His companions laughed rudely, and Darcy had walked a little faster.

A terrible thought clawed at Darcy. Maybe she was the loser, not Tarah. Tarah was always hanging with a bunch of kids, laughing and joking. She would go down the hall to the lockers and greetings would come from everywhere. "Hey, Tarah!" "What's up, Tar?" "See ya at lunch, girl." When Darcy went to the lockers, there was dead silence.

Darcy usually glanced into stores on her way home from school. She enjoyed looking at the trays of chicken feet and pork ears at the little Asian grocery store. Sometimes she would even steal a glance at the diners sitting by the picture window at the Golden Grill Restaurant. But today she stared straight ahead, her shoulders drooping.

If this had happened last year, she would have gone directly to Grandma's house, a block from where Darcy lived. How many times had Darcy and Jamee run to Grandma's, eaten applesauce cookies, drunk cider, and poured out their troubles to Grandma. Somehow, their problems would always dissolve in the warmth of her love and wisdom. But now Grandma was a frail figure in the corner of their apartment, saying little. And what little she did say made less and less sense.

Darcy was usually the first one home. The minute she got there, Mom left for the hospital to take the 3:00 to 11:00 shift in the ER. By the time Mom finished her paperwork at the hospital, she would be lucky to be home again by midnight. After Mom left, Darcy went to Grandma's room to give her the malted nutrition drink that the doctor ordered her to have three times a day.

"Want to drink your chocolate malt, Grandma?" Darcy asked, pulling up a chair beside Grandma's bed.

Grandma was sitting up, and her eyes were open. "No. I'm not hungry," she said listlessly. She always said that.

"You need to drink your malt, Grandma," Darcy insisted, gently putting the straw between the pinched lips.

Grandma sucked the malt slowly. "Grandma, nobody likes me at school," Darcy said. She did not expect any response. But there was a strange comfort in telling Grandma anyway. "Everybody laughs at me. It's because I'm shy and maybe stuck-up, too, I guess. But I don't mean to be. Stuck-up, I mean. Maybe I'm weird. I could be weird, I guess. I could be like Aunt Charlotte . . ." Tears rolled down Darcy's cheeks. Her heart ached with loneliness. There was nobody to talk to anymore, nobody who had time to listen, nobody who understood.

Grandma blinked and pushed the straw away. Her eyes brightened as they did now and then. "You are a wonderful girl. Everybody knows that," Grandma said in an almost normal voice. It happened like that sometimes. It was like being in the middle of a dark storm and having the clouds part, revealing a patch of clear, sunlit blue. For just a few precious minutes, Grandma was bright-eyed and saying normal things.

"Oh, Grandma, I'm so lonely," Darcy cried, pressing her head against Grandma's small shoulder.

"You were such a beautiful baby," Grandma said, stroking her hair." 'That one is going to shine like the morning star.' That's what I told your Mama. 'That child is going to shine like the morning star.' Tell me, Angelcake, is your daddy home yet?"

Darcy straightened. "Not yet." Her heart pounded so hard, she could feel it thumping in her chest. Darcy's father had not been home in five years.

"Well, tell him to see me when he gets home. I want him to buy you that blue dress you liked in the store window. That's for you, Angelcake. Tell him I've got money. My social security came, you know. I have money for the blue dress," Grandma said, her eyes slipping shut.

Just then, Darcy heard the apartment door slam. Jamee had come home. Now she stood in the hall, her hands belligerently on her hips. "Are you talking to Grandma again?" Jamee demanded.

"She was talking like normal," Darcy said. "Sometimes she does. You know she does."

"That is so stupid," Jamee snapped. "She never says anything right anymore. Not anything!" Jamee's voice trembled.

Darcy got up quickly and set down the can of malted milk. She ran to Jamee and put her arms around her sister. "Jamee, I know you're hurting too."

"Oh, don't be stupid," Jamee protested, but Darcy hugged her more tightly, and in a few seconds Jamee was crying. "She was the best thing in this stupid house," Jamee cried. "Why'd she have to go?"

"She didn't go," Darcy said. "Not really."

"She did! She did!" Jamee sobbed. She struggled free of Darcy, ran to her room, and slammed the door. In a minute, Darcy heard the bone-rattling sound of rap music.

Lost and Found, *a Bluford Series*™ *novel, is reprinted with permission from Townsend Press. Copyright © 2002.*

Want to read more? This and other *Bluford Series*™ novels and paperbacks can be purchased for $1 each at www.townsendpress.com.

Teens:
How to Get More Out of This Book

Self-help: The teens who wrote the stories in this book did so because they hope that telling their stories will help readers who are facing similar challenges. They want you to know that you are not alone, and that taking specific steps can help you manage or overcome very difficult situations. They've done their best to be clear about the actions that worked for them so you can see if they'll work for you.

Writing: You can also use the book to improve your writing skills. Each teen in this book wrote 5-10 drafts of his or her story before it was published. If you read the stories closely you'll see that the teens work to include a beginning, a middle, and an end, and good scenes, description, dialogue, and anecdotes (little stories). To improve your writing, take a look at how these writers construct their stories. Try some of their techniques in your own writing.

Reading: Finally, you'll notice that we include the first chapter from a Bluford Series novel in this book, alongside the true stories by teens. We hope you'll like it enough to continue reading. The more you read, the more you'll strengthen your reading skills. Teens at Youth Communication like the Bluford novels because they explore themes similar to those in their own stories. Your school may already have the Bluford books. If not, you can order them online for only $1.

Resources on the Web

We will occasionally post Think About It questions on our website, www.youthcomm.org, to accompany stories in this and other Youth Communication books. We try out the questions with teens and post the ones they like best. Many teens report that writing answers to those questions in a journal is very helpful.

How to Use This Book in Staff Training

Staff say that reading these stories gives them greater insight into what teens are thinking and feeling, and new strategies for working with them. You can help the staff you work with by using these stories as case studies.

Select one story to read in the group, and ask staff to identify and discuss the main issue facing the teen. There may be disagreement about this, based on the background and experience of staff. That is fine. One point of the exercise is that teens have complex lives and needs. Adults can probably be more effective if they don't focus too narrowly and can see several dimensions of their clients.

Ask staff: What issues or feelings does the story provoke in them? What kind of help do they think the teen wants? What interventions are likely to be most promising? Least effective? Why? How would you build trust with the teen writer? How have other adults failed the teen, and how might that affect his or her willingness to accept help? What other resources would be helpful to this teen, such as peer support, a mentor, counseling, family therapy, etc.

Resources on the Web

From time to time we will post Think About It questions on our website, www.youthcomm.org, to accompany stories in this and other Youth Communication books. We try out the questions with teens and post the ones that they find most effective. We'll also post lesson for some of the stories. Adults can use the questions and lessons in workshops.

> **Discussion Guide**

Teachers and Staff:
How to Use This Book in Groups

When working with teens individually or in groups, using these stories can help young people face difficult issues in a way that feels safe to them. That's because talking about the issues in the stories usually feels safer to teens than talking about those same issues in their own lives. Addressing issues through the stories allows for some personal distance; they hit close to home, but not too close. Talking about them opens up a safe place for reflection. As teens gain confidence talking about the issues in the stories, they usually become more comfortable talking about those issues in their own lives.

Below are general questions that can help you lead discussions about the stories, which help teens and staff reflect on the issues in their own work and lives. In most cases you can read a story and conduct a discussion in one 45-minute session. Teens are usually happy to read the stories aloud, with each teen reading a paragraph or two. (Allow teens to pass if they don't want to read.) It takes 10-15 minutes to read a story straight through. However, it is often more effective to let workshop participants make comments and discuss the story as you go along. The workshop leader may even want to annotate her copy of the story beforehand with key questions.

If teens read the story ahead of time or silently, it's good to break the ice with a few questions that get everyone on the same page: Who is the main character? How old is she? What happened to her? How did she respond? Etc. Another good starting question is: "What stood out for you in the story?" Go around the room and let each person briefly mention one thing.

Then move on to open-ended questions, which encourage participants to think more deeply about what the writers were feeling, the choices they faced, and they actions they took. There are no right or wrong answers to the open-ended questions. Open-ended questions encourage participants to think about how the themes, emotions and choices in the stories relate to their own lives. Here are some examples of open-ended questions that we have found to be effective. You can use variations of these questions with almost any story in this book.

—What main problem or challenge did the writer face?

—What choices did the teen have in trying to deal with the problem?

—Which way of dealing with the problem was most effective for the teen? Why?

—What strengths, skills, or resources did the teen use to address the challenge?

—If you were in the writer's shoes, what would you have done?

—What could adults have done better to help this young person?

—What have you learned by reading this story that you didn't know before?

—What, if anything, will you do differently after reading this story?

—What surprised you in this story?

—Do you have a different view of this issue, or see a different way of dealing with it, after reading this story? Why or why not?

Credits

The stories in this book originally appeared in the following Youth Communication publications:

"Am I Ready For Love?" by Hattie Rice, *Represent*, May/June 2007

"Just the Two of Us," by Oumar Bowman, *Represent*, September/October 2000

"Making a Fairy Tale Out of a Man," by Anonymous, *Represent*, July/August 2005

"When the Past Pops Up, Pay Attention," by Natasha Santos, *Represent*, July/August 2005

"Opening Up to My Shorty," by Antwaun Garcia, *Represent*, January/February 2003

"Reaching Out to My Enemy" by Chantel Clark, *Represent*, November/December 2002

"Want a Friend? Be a Friend!" by Antwaun Garcia, *Represent*, January/February 2005

"My Sister and Me," by Cynthia Orbes, *Represent*, November/December 2008

"Loving and Losing," by Anonymous, *Represent*, May/June 2007

"Black and Blue," by Zoraida Medina, *Represent*, May/June 2000

"How Do You Find A Healthy Relationship?" *Represent*, November/December 2008

"For Love or Money," by Erica Harrigan, *Represent*, July/August 2005

"Player No More," by Rosheed Wellington, *New Youth Connections*, November 2005

"In Search of Myself" by Seandrea Evans, *Represent*, January/February 2003

"My First Friend," by Hattie Rice, *Represent*, January/February 2005

"Playing To Win," by Fred Wagenhauser, *Represent*, May/June 2007

"Learning to Love Again," by Shaniqua Sockwell, *Represent*, January/February 2004

About Youth Communication

Youth Communication, founded in 1980, is a nonprofit youth development program located in New York City whose mission is to teach writing, journalism, and leadership skills. The teenagers we train become writers for our websites and books and for two print magazines, *New Youth Connections*, a general-interest youth magazine, and *Represent*, a magazine by and for young people in foster care.

Each year, up to 100 young people participate in Youth Communication's school-year and summer journalism workshops where they work under the direction of full-time professional editors. Most are African American, Latino, or Asian, and many are recent immigrants. The opportunity to reach their peers with accurate portrayals of their lives and important self-help information motivates the young writers to create powerful stories.

Our goal is to run a strong youth development program in which teens produce high quality stories that inform and inspire their peers. Doing so requires us to be sensitive to the complicated lives and emotions of the teen participants while also providing an intellectually rigorous experience. We achieve that goal in the writing/teaching/editing relationship, which is the core of our program.

Our teaching and editorial process begins with discussions

between adult editors and the teen staff. In those meetings, the teens and the editors work together to identify the most important issues in the teens' lives and to figure out how those issues can be turned into stories that will resonate with teen readers.

Once story topics are chosen, students begin the process of crafting their stories. For a personal story, that means revisiting events in one's past to understand their significance for the future. For a commentary, it means developing a logical and persuasive point of view. For a reported story, it means gathering information through research and interviews. Students look inward and outward as they try to make sense of their experiences and the world around them and find the points of intersection between personal and social concerns. That process can take a few weeks or a few months. Stories frequently go through ten or more drafts as students work under the guidance of their editors, the way any professional writer does.

Many of the students who walk through our doors have uneven skills, as a result of poor education, living under extremely stressful conditions, or coming from homes where English is a second language. Yet, to complete their stories, students must successfully perform a wide range of activities, including writing and rewriting, reading, discussion, reflection, research, interviewing, and typing. They must work as members of a team and they must accept individual responsibility. They learn to provide constructive criticism, and to accept it. They engage in explorations of truthfulness, fairness, and accuracy. They meet deadlines. They must develop the audacity to believe that they have something important to say and the humility to recognize that saying it well is not a process of instant gratification. Rather, it usually requires a long, hard struggle through many discussions and much rewriting.

It would be impossible to teach these skills and dispositions as separate, disconnected topics, like grammar, ethics, or assertiveness. However, we find that students make rapid progress when they are learning skills in the context of an inquiry that is personally significant to them and that will benefit their peers.

When teens publish their stories—in *New Youth Connections* and *Represent*, on the web, and in other publications—they reach tens of thousands of teen and adult readers. Teachers, counselors, social workers, and other adults circulate the stories to young people in their classes and out-of-school youth programs. Adults tell us that teens in their programs—including many who are ordinarily resistant to reading—clamor for the stories. Teen readers report that the stories give them information they can't get anywhere else, and inspire them to reflect on their lives and open lines of communication with adults.

Writers usually participate in our program for one semester, though some stay much longer. Years later, many of them report that working here was a turning point in their lives—that it helped them acquire the confidence and skills that they needed for success in college and careers. Scores of our graduates have overcome tremendous obstacles to become journalists, writers, and novelists. They include National Book Award finalist Edwidge Danticat, novelist Ernesto Quinonez, writer Veronica Chambers and *New York Times* reporter Rachel Swarns. Hundreds more are working in law, business, and other careers. Many are teachers, principals, and youth workers, and several have started nonprofit youth programs themselves and work as mentors—helping another generation of young people develop their skills and find their voices.

Youth Communication is a nonprofit educational corporation. Contributions are gratefully accepted and are tax deductible to the fullest extent of the law.

To make a contribution, or for information about our publications and programs, including our catalog of over 100 books and curricula for hard-to-reach teens, see www.youthcomm.org

About The Editors

Al Desetta has been an editor of Youth Communication's two teen magazines, *Foster Care Youth United* (now known as *Represent*) and *New Youth Connections*. He was also an instructor in Youth Communication's juvenile prison writing program. In 1991, he became the organization's first director of teacher development, working with high school teachers to help them produce better writers and student publications.

Prior to working at Youth Communication, Desetta directed environmental education projects in New York City public high schools and worked as a reporter.

He has a master's degree in English literature from City College of the City University of New York and a bachelor's degree from the State University of New York at Binghamton, and he was a Revson Fellow at Columbia University for the 1990-91 academic year.

He is the editor of many books, including several other Youth Communication anthologies: *The Heart Knows Something Different: Teenage Voices from the Foster Care System*, *The Struggle to Be Strong*, and *The Courage to Be Yourself*. He is currently a freelance editor.

Keith Hefner co-founded Youth Communication in 1980 and has directed it ever since. He is the recipient of the Luther P. Jackson Education Award from the New York Association of Black Journalists and a MacArthur Fellowship. He was also a Revson Fellow at Columbia University.

Laura Longhine is the editorial director at Youth Communication. She edited *Represent*, Youth Communication's magazine by and for youth in foster care, for three years, and has written for a variety of publications. She has a BA in English from Tufts University and an MS in Journalism from Columbia University.

More Helpful Books From Youth Comunication

Do You Have What It Takes? A Comprehensive Guide to Success After Foster Care. In this survival manual, current and former foster teens show how they prepared not only for the practical challenges they've faced on the road to independence, but also the emotional ones. Worksheets and exercises help foster teens plan for their future. Activity pages at the end of each chapter help social workers, independent living instructors, and other leaders use the stories with individuals or in groups. (Youth Communication)

The Struggle to Be Strong: True Stories by Teens About Overcoming Tough Times. Foreword by Veronica Chambers. Help young people identify and build on their own strengths with 30 personal stories about resiliency. (Free Spirit)

Depression, Anger, Sadness: Teens Write About Facing Difficult Emotions. Give teens the confidence they need to seek help when they need it. These teens write candidly about difficult emotional problems—such as depression, cutting, and domestic violence—and how they have tried to help themselves. (Youth Communication)

What Staff Need to Know: Teens Write About What Works. How can foster parents, group home staff, caseworkers, social workers, and teachers best help teens? These stories show how communication can be improved on both sides, and provide insight into what kinds of approaches and styles work best. (Youth Communication)

Haunted By My Past: Teens Write About Surviving Sexual Abuse. Help teens feel less alone and more hopeful about overcoming the trauma of sexual abuse. This collection includes first-person accounts by male and female survivors grappling with fear, shame, and guilt. (Youth Communication)

The Fury Inside: Teens Write About Anger. Help teens manage their anger. These writers show how they got better control of their emotions and sought the support of others. (Youth Communication)

Always on the Move: Teens Write About Changing Homes and Staff. Help teens feel less alone with these stories about how their peers have coped with the painful experience of frequent placement changes, and turnover among staff and social workers. (Youth Communication)

 *Two Moms in My Heart: Teens Write About the Adoption Option.* Teens will appreciate these stories by peers who describe how complicated the adoption experience can be—even when it should give them a more stable home than foster care. (Youth Communication)

My Secret Addiction: Teens Write About Cutting. These true accounts of cutting, or self-mutilation, offer a window into the personal and family situations that lead to this secret habit, and show how teens can get the help they need. (Youth Communication)

 *Growing Up Together: Teens Write About Being Parents.* Give teens a realistic view of the conflicts and burdens of parenthood with these stories from real teen parents. The stories also reveal how teens grew as individuals by struggling to become responsible parents. (Youth Communication)

To order these and other books, go to:
www.youthcomm.org
or call 212-279-0708 x115

www.ingramcontent.com/pod-product-compliance
Lightning Source LLC
Chambersburg PA
CBHW071729090426
42738CB00011B/2424